THAT'S WHY THEY CALL IT PRACTICE

EDWARD (DR. ED) MIGNECO, DVM

ISBN: 979-8-218-35704-7

Design by Jill Halpin

Printed in the United States of America
23 24 25 26 27   5 4 3 2 1

Dedication

I would like to dedicate this book to Nicole. You came into my life at a time when I was doubting myself and my self-worth. You saw something in me and believed in me when I needed it the most, and stuck with me through my trials and tribulations. You inspired and encouraged me to pick up my writing again and were a source of strength. I am very lucky to have been given a second chance at love and I plan on living the rest of my life to the fullest with you. Thank you very much and I love you.

Foreword

Dr. Edward Migneco has devoted his career and life to helping animals in need. We have had the privilege of personally experiencing his craft and expertise on numerous occasions, both with our menagerie of cherished family pets and those who are not as lucky–the animals that have been cast off and abandoned by our society and have gone on to survive some of the most unimaginable circumstances.

The personal care and attention to detail Dr. Ed gave to each of his clients came with a healthy dose of affection and humor, but the level of knowledge he was known to deliver about a particular health concern or issue was always top notch. We have many fond memories of his dedication to both people and their pets. We experienced him do home visits with one of our more tricky or, better said, "not easy to treat" dogs that had a long history of abuse and neglect; he and his team swiftly rushed to help during a midnight cesarean section on a dog our family was fostering, who would have otherwise likely died on the street; and he often provided steeply discounted services for shelter and rescue groups and people who would otherwise be forced to surrender their animals.

Dr. Ed displays humanity and generosity that demonstrates excellence on all levels.

This book tells his side of the stories collated from more than 30 years in practice and from the inside of his sought-after veterinary practice in the heart of St. Louis. It will give you a behind-the-scenes look at an array of situations, circumstances, and understanding not many have personally seen. Dr. Ed tells the real, raw, and rarely heard stories from the other side of the examination table. Tales of everything from harrowing rescues and outlandish clients to poignant family matters are delivered with humor and lots of learning by one of the most caring, personable, knowledgeable, and skilled people we have met. Get ready to be inspired as you turn the pages of this book in utter disbelief. We have a feeling you will certainly be entertained and enlightened by the true and remarkable moments from a career of caring.

"Unless someone like you
cares a whole awful lot,
nothing is going to change, it's just not"

– Dr. Seuss, book – The Lorax

-Kelly and David Backes

THAT'S WHY THEY CALL IT PRACTICE

Preface

As I was gathering my thoughts and starting to put together this book, my mind was brought back to the many times I was having lunch with my veterinary friends, relating the good and bad times as we allowed each other to vent about our day or week. I have always joked that we all seem to have the same clients, just "the names have been changed to protect the innocent." The first of many TV and movie references in the book. Most of these stories are from my personal experiences at Hillside Animal Hospital and the various rescue organizations I have either volunteered for or worked for over the course of my career. Interspersed are some family stories to give you some insight into my background. I have also included a few stories related to me by some of my friends in the veterinary community, to show that what has happened to me is not a set of unique circumstances, but is probably happening again and again across the country in veterinary clinics. Included in the book are several shorter writings I call Musings, which are not complete stories, just smaller bits of random thoughts and ideas, shared between chapters. I was lucky enough to start writing down some of these stories as they happened in an effort to remember them and that has eventually led to this book. I hope you enjoy reading it as much as I have enjoyed reliving these moments.

THAT'S WHY THEY CALL IT PRACTICE

A lot of things can happen during the course of a single day in a veterinary practice that may end up absolutely ruining your day. You could be urinated on, defecated on, sprayed with anal sac material, bit, scratched, or any combination thereof. And it's not just the animals interfering with a smooth-sailing work day. Your employees could do something to ruin your day, or a mistake of your own doing makes you wish it were tomorrow already.

Whenever something happens like this to me, I know I can always call one of my veterinary friends to help cheer me up. I can call Mark across town, Ross across the state, or Matt across the country, and they usually tell me how the same thing has happened to them at one time or another. This is reassuring, especially if I think that I've made a mistake managing a particular case. I am sure I am like other veterinarians in that we are always hardest on ourselves.

When I am having a bad day my friend Mark is especially helpful. Many a time I have called him, feeling very depressed about something that happened or something I did wrong. I might have dropped an ovarian pedicle during a spay surgery and made the surgery more difficult and longer that it needed to be. Or I might have overlooked an obvious electrolyte disorder which would have made a diagnosis a lot easier and saved my patient some distress from vomiting. I always come away feeling better; because sometimes it is just a matter of vocalizing the issue in order to get it off your chest. Knowing that one of your colleagues has made the same mistake, or had the same bad thing happen, can really

help your state of mind and stop you from beating yourself up about the mistake. I've returned the favor by lending an ear for venting when needed.

I have been practicing as a veterinarian for over 30 years. I was very fortunate and bought a practice in my own neighborhood of St. Louis where I had started working during high school. Up until recently I owned that practice, and decided it was time to move on and start the second phase of my career so that I may pursue my lifelong passion of helping out animal welfare organizations. I sold the practice to my daughter and her spouse. Not too many people can say that about their practice. I am very proud to have them continue on the tradition that is Hillside Animal Hospital. Now I am a semi-retired veterinarian, and I am working for one of the animal rescue/animal welfare organizations that I had volunteered for in the past. It's important to me to continuing doing the work that I have done my entire career, helping out animals and their owners.

I have always written funny stories and anecdotes that have occurred during the course of practicing veterinary medicine. I looked upon it as a way to help preserve the art of practice in my life and to show other vets that we all share common stories. I have rewritten and edited my stories several times along the way. Now here I am at the stage of publishing them as one collection. My goal in this project is to donate the profits to the important animal groups that I've worked with in the past, as well as those I will be continue to work with in the future. Trying to write a book is not an easy process, and getting it published after it is written is another difficult step. There were many times I struggled with the writing and wondered what the heck was I thinking in trying to write a book. I have had several ideas for the title but I kept coming back to my good friend Mark's admonition about the trials of life as a veterinarian whenever I had the occasion to call him up when I was feeling down. "That's why they call it practice." That good advice applies to life in general, as well as to my chosen profession.

DR.ED STORIES

VOMIT CONTROL OFFICER

When it comes to animal care at our house, I've always been the final authority. Being the only veterinarian in the house, any time one of our pets had any problem, my family turned to me. I'm responsible for Jack the dog, and cats Coal, Helen, and Tuxie's medical care and most of the feedings. But I don't recall anything in the veterinary oath about being the only one who's able to clean up after them.

I have three lovely daughters. As they grew up, naturally there were times when they threw up. Babies throw up all the time and no one ever worries about it. People even think it's cute when a baby throws up sour milk on you and ruins your brand-new shirt. But it has always been difficult for me to deal with human vomit. I have never enjoyed being awakened in the middle of the night by the sound of a child vomiting.

There is a completely different dynamic if one of the pets vomits. The sound of a cat retching up a hairball has been known to ruin many a night's sleep or family dinner. All heads would automatically turn towards me and say in unison, "Dad, the cat just threw up." In other words, "Dad, clean up after your pet." In no time, I had become the animal vomit control officer of my family. I guess a baby vomiting is a lot cuter to some people than a cat hacking up a hairball in the middle of the night. I don't think I would enjoy discovering either with my bare feet though.

I think I know when this title and its responsibilities were bestowed upon me. After the birth of my first daughter Anna, I was not the parent who usually got up in the middle of the night when Anna called room service. I tried for a while to say it was because I could not breast feed her, but that excuse only lasted as long as the breast feeding did. After that, middle of the night feedings was fair game for either of us.

One night though it was Anna's mom who answered the call of the wild child, and got up to feed her. Now it just so happened that we had a new puppy in the house, and it decided that this middle of the night interruption meant it was time for him to go outside. So, picture this please. There's Anna's mom, holding a crying baby in her arms as she

tries to get her to take the bottle, and there's the puppy, acting all excited and whining to be let outside.

Trying to do multiple things at one time did not work out so well, because as she tried to get up from the rocking chair to let the puppy out the back door into the yard, the young pup decided it had waited long enough and started to defecate right near the back door. Anna's mom jumped up and opened the door, which then proceeded to smear the dog poop all over the carpet. Did I mention Anna was still crying? By this point, I believe everyone involved was crying also.

The icing on the cake was that despite all the commotion of a crying baby, pooping puppy, and messy carpet, I somehow managed to remain asleep the entire time. I woke up very refreshed in the morning, but I could not understand why Anna and her mom did not. Boy, did I hear about it. Of course, I only heard about after I removed my ear plugs that I use for sleeping.

FULL OF BALONEY

We were rechecking out a dog at the clinic because it could not hold down the medicine that we had sent home for a particular problem. The owners said he vomited every time he received a dose of the medicine. We had told them to stop the medicine, but we still wanted to see the dog to examine him again and see what we could do for him. While at the clinic for the day for observation, he vomited in his cage and in the vomitus were whole pieces of bologna. When we noticed this, I immediately starting singing, "My vomit has a first name, it's O-S-C-A-R......
My vomit has a second name it's M-E-Y-E-R, because Oscar Meyer has a way with N-A-U-S-E-A.

IT'S A LIVING

When you do what I do for a living, it is not uncommon for people you meet in social situations to ask you questions about their pets. I always enjoy these moments, because it affords me a connection with a person that I might not have had otherwise. Some people do not like to talk shop when they are not working, but I do not want to pass up the chance to connect with someone and talk about pets, which are such an important part of our lives. Occasionally the fact that I am a veterinarian has escaped the notice of some people that I am meeting, and this can make for some uncomfortable moments.

At a social gathering one night, I was enjoying myself right up until I met one of the guests named Wayne. He immediately said, "Oh, I heard about you. You must be the butcher." Some of the people who were there knew what I did for a living, and they started to chuckle a little bit. Wayne looked confused and did not realize what was wrong. I finally confessed to him what was so funny, and he felt a little sheepish. Not to worry, I said. I hope no one ever calls me that for real, considering my job.

I try to work out at the local YMCA several mornings a week, before heading home for breakfast and then to work. At that early hour there are regular members who have the same routine as I do. In the evenings after work the gym is a lot more crowded and less personable. The early birds get to be a little friendlier, because there are fewer of us. One particular gentleman always made it a point to tell me to have a good day, as it seemed we would be leaving about the same time. Then one week, he changed things up and said, "Knock' em dead today." He did this for a couple more days until I finally confided in him what I did for a living. Of course, he felt self-conscious, but I told him that it was not a problem. I said that every time he told me that, I would go to work and hope that I did not have to knock anyone dead that day.

As a matter of fact, I think there ought to be a law that you cannot say, "Break a leg," or "Knock' em dead," to a veterinarian. Try "Save a life," or "Spay a cat," instead. Much more encouraging.

SOCIAL DISTANCING

An outcome of the restrictions seen during the height of the pandemic, which has still carried over to become an almost routine part of our daily lives, is the Zoom Meeting. I know that after a while all of the Zoom meetings got be a little tiresome. It is easy to feel disconnected, even if we are connected virtually with others through our computers. At veterinary clinics, at least in the beginning of the pandemic, clients were usually kept outside in their cars, and communication was done virtually or over the phone lines concerning the care for their pets. This disconnect of doctor-client-patient interaction also took its toll on all of us. Since the pandemic has slowed down and we are back to allowing clients into the clinic, the visits are a lot more enjoyable, not only with the interaction with the pets, but also the face-to-face interaction with the clients again. But I recently had a visit with a client and their new puppy for a wellness examination and vaccinations at the clinic that reinforced how much the Zoom meeting had become ingrained into our daily routine. This particular puppy was very cute and lively and as expected it was an enjoyable visit for all of us involved. I have always said that new puppy and kitten visits are my favorite part of my job. Who doesn't love that "puppy breath" smell? This recent simple appointment with this new puppy combined the idea of a Zoom meeting with the face-to-face interaction that we all crave. You see, this puppy's name was Zoom. This was the first Zoom meeting where I got licked on the face.

M U S I N G S

CLOTHES HOUND

I have never been accused of being the best dresser in the world. That does not mean I am a bad dresser, just not a slave to fashion. At the clinic I personally prefer to not wear a tie or even a lab coat while seeing appointments. I think they are just attractants for urine, feces, or anal sac material. My usual attire is nice slacks and a button-down shirt, but I guess after being attacked at the clinic and attacked in the washing machine, my clothes have been known occasionally to be worse for wear. As I have gotten older I sometimes wear scrub tops and pants for appointments as well as surgery. Maybe this story had something to do with that trend.

The opposite is true on the occasions I attend a continuing education conference, where I enjoy dressing up in my "reserved" nice clothes, including sport coats and ties. I even have a collection of very fashionable ties, notably from the Jerry Garcia collection. You may know him as the deceased leader of the Grateful Dead, but a collection of silk ties was also fashioned after his artwork. He also has lent his name to a nice flavor of ice cream. On occasion I have been known to wear one of my Three Stooges ties with my crisp ensemble, and I routinely get compliments on all these ties.

My staff are usually my unofficial fashion critics, complimenting me when I look good, or come in wearing something new that I have bought. They can be just as critical also, in a nice way, when my clothes are becoming too worn, and they also remind me that it may be time to retire a favorite shirt. Just because there is an ink stain on the front pocket? I hate throwing away an otherwise perfectly good shirt.

One routine day at work, one of my patients became my fashion critic. One of my very good clients was coming in for a behavioral consultation. One of her dogs, known to be aggressive, was becoming even harder for her to handle. I know this client well, and she has adopted dogs in the past with behavioral issues. She is a dedicated owner and works hard with these dogs but this particular dog was becoming too much for even her to handle. My staff had situated her and her dog in a larger exam

room used for behavioral consultations.

As I entered, the owner was standing in the middle of the room holding the dog's leash. I had barely entered the room and said hello to the client when the dog suddenly leapt ferociously at me. It was one of those attacks that happen so suddenly and viciously, you are strictly in survival mode. The dog jumped right at my groin area, but luckily for me the owner still had hold of the leash. I ended up on the floor but very quickly picked myself up, and got back out the door which was right behind me.

After I got outside the door into the hallway I basically collapsed after the adrenaline rush that had just occurred. My staff had heard my primal yell and had come running. They helped me to my feet and then pointed out that my pants had been split open from my groin all the way down to my shoes. I had not even noticed my torn pants yet. I had escaped without a scratch, but I couldn't help but think what would have happened if the dog had reached just an inch further with his teeth. It took me quite a while to regain my composure and settle down.

Believe it or not, I still had to deal with the dog after this scene. I changed into some scrub pants and carefully re-entered the room. The client had control of the dog and was as upset as I was over what had occurred. I assured her that I was okay, and that it was not her fault. She had been on the fence about the possible need to euthanize this dog due to its behavioral issues, and needless to say this incident had made up her mind. Since I had escaped without any bites or scratches, we did proceed with the euthanasia in a very humane fashion, with as little stress as possible for the client or the dog.

After the incident I finished the day working in my scrub pants. My staff wanted me to keep the torn pants around as a reminder of what had almost happened, but I could not throw them away fast enough. I did not need to be reminded of what I had almost lost. From that day forward, whenever one of my staff members would gently point out that I had a hole or snag in one of my pants I would remind them of the pants from that portentous day. I guess maybe the dog just didn't like my pants, or thought they were too old or faded to be worn any more. It seems everybody is a critic.

I GOT THE MUSIC IN ME

I really like music. Music is an important part of my life. I cannot play a lick or carry a tune, and the only singing I do is in the car by myself. I am prone to say that I can play a mean radio. You will not find me listening to talk radio in the car, or when doing surgery or exercising. When I get together with some of my friends, I may not be able to add to the conversation when they mention what Wolf-what's-his-name said on his radio show, but I would be happy to comment on the Rolling Stones, who I finally got to see live in concert. More on that later.

Early in my career when I was still practicing in my original building, we were a little cramped for space as the practice grew. The building was only 1200 square feet and the exam room doubled as the surgery room for some time. I would usually do surgeries over the lunch hour, and it was not unusual to have the clinic radio tuned to KSHE-95, Real Rock Radio. KSHE was and still is an institution in the St. Louis area and is well-known elsewhere. It is considered the classic rock station, so the music was right up my alley. The radio actually sat outside the doorway of the surgery room but the building was so small it was very easy to hear. No iPads, SiriusXM, speakers the size of a deck of cards, or even small headphones were available in the '80s. So, if I wanted to listen to The Who or Led Zeppelin during surgery, everyone in the clinic did also.

One afternoon after lunchtime, we were getting ready to see appointments. I was cleaning up the exam/surgical room and sneaked a peek in the waiting room. Sitting in one of the chairs was a young male teen with shoulder-length scraggly hair, wearing a black, heavy metal concert T-shirt of some kind, with one of those chains hanging out of his front pocket attached to his ratty jeans. If I had to venture a guess, I think the T-shirt was MegaDeath or Iron Maiden for all I know. My mind started to form some preconceived notions about this kid, which was leading me to think that I would not be enjoying this next appointment. I could see the teenage angst and rebellion written all over his face and knew that nothing I would say could appease this young punk.

I finally finished cleaning up and invited this Kelly Leak wannabe into

the exam room. Go ahead. I dare you to look up that movie reference. I hope it makes you smile. I could have said James Dean wannabe but that would have limited the laughs to a much, much older crowd. Holding a small shoe box in his lap, he slowly stood up and entered the room, keeping his head down and not looking up to establish eye contact with me. He stood unsteadily in front of the exam table, clutching the shoe box to his chest. I introduced myself, and asked what I could do for him today.

After a few seconds of awkward silence, he continued to hold his head down, and I thought I heard very faint sobbing going on. I couldn't tell for sure but he may have been crying a few tears. I tried a different tack and gently asked who he had brought with him today for me to see. He finally spoke in a hushed tone, interspersed with some sniffles and sobs. The conversation went on like this. "It's my guinea pig, Fluffy. He's very sick." Following a heavy sigh, he continued, "He's not eating at all." Finally, he broke down. "I think he's dying." As this was going on I became acutely aware that I had left the radio on outside the exam room following surgery. I could hear Derek and the Dominos singing "Layla" out in the hallway as I asked the young boy if I could take the box from him to examine his beloved pet. Everything about the appointment then changed in the blink of an eye.

As he was handing me the box, he said in between more tears, "I don't know what I am going to do." Then he stopped sobbing, cocked his head towards the sound coming from the other door, and said 'Hey, cool song." Well, that broke the ice between us and we connected thanks to Eric Clapton. I cannot honestly say that the news was good for Fluffy. After learning what was wrong with Fluffy, the young man understood that there were some serious problems that no one could fix. While sad, he was able to keep it together and mature enough to allow me to do what was best for his beloved friend. Thankfully in this case music was a way of bringing people together, especially after my wrongful first impressions. It was fortuitous that the radio had been left on.

Fast forward some 30 years now. During 2020 it was announced that the Rolling Stones were going on tour again and were in fact stopping in St. Louis. I had always dreamed of going to see them in concert, but

had missed out on several chances in the past. I jumped at the chance and purchased four rather expensive tickets. I was not going to miss my chance again. Lo and behold, Covid-19 happened and the concert was cancelled. I was greatly disappointed, but understood the reality of the situation.

A couple of months before leaving the country on a safari to Africa, it was announced that the Stones were resuming their tour. Unfortunately, the rescheduled date for St. Louis was while I would be in Africa. I felt snake-bit. Twice the chance to finally see them was pulled out from underneath me. I mean, I know that Africa was going to be fantastic, but The Rolling Stones. C'mon man!

Well, I went online and found out that one of their tour stops was in Nashville. So, I purchased tickets for the concert which was scheduled only four days after I returned from Africa. Jet lag be damned. This time I purchased tickets for myself, my fiancée Nicole, and two of my daughters and their significant others. The concert exceeded all my expectations as I finally got to see Mick Jagger singing "Start Me Up" along with all of the great classic Stones' hits. They sure don't act or sing like they are in their late 70s. And to be able to experience it with my daughters and Nicole was extra special. I hope I did not embarrass them by singing or dancing too much. Not that I cared.

I maybe the only person in the world who went trekking to see the mountain gorillas in Uganda and saw The Rolling Stones in concert all within six days. That's how important music is to me.

My fiancée, Dr. Nicole Fulcher, and myself at the Rolling Stones Concert in Nashville (2021)

Mountain gorillas in Uganda (2021)

BITE ME

Considering our staff works closely with patients containing sharp teeth and claws, the risk of injury is inherent in the veterinary profession. Some animal patients turn sour after being woken up from a nap and being brought to the clinic with its strange smells and other fearful stimuli. Then to top it all off, they are sometimes jabbed in the rear with needles. We do our best to make sure each animal that comes into the clinic is provided the least stressful environment and handling as possible but it is not always enough to calm the anxieties of the patients, or even the owners. Our staff makes sure to ask the owner about their animal's temperament and muzzle options if we think the patient in question is fearful or aggressive. Most clients don't mind when we inquire about muzzle usage, but occasionally someone will object. I do my best to explain that though their animal might be docile and friendly at home, they easily could lash out of fear when being poked and prodded, then adding that I'm accountable for the safety of not only my staff but also my clients. An upset animal can bite or scratch whomever they're closest to.

A relatively new product that our staff had become quite fond of looks like a flea collar, but it releases a pheromone instead of an insecticide. A pheromone is similar to a hormone, but it's released outside of the body, is detectable by another animal of the same species, and it can have an effect, ranging from sexual attraction to warning of possible danger. Pheromones don't produce a smell, but their presence is detected by the body of the receiving party on a physiological level. This particular product contained the pheromone aptly named Dog Appeasing Pheromone (DAP), one of the first veterinary-specific products for treating anxiety.

DAP is the pheromone a mother dog secretes when she is nursing puppies. I became a proponent after studying the research data behind this product. The company that developed this product took several litters of puppies and divided each litter into groups at the time of weaning, which is when the pups were taken away from their mother and each other. One group of pups was sent to their new homes with DAP collars, and the other group was sent without collars. The study

group with no collars acted just as would be expected new puppies being weaned to act. They whined and cried all night because they were in new environments and missed their moms, and siblings. The study group with the DAP collars on mostly slept through the night and appeared not to suffer from weaning anxiety. No product like this should be expected to be 100% effective, but I was eager to try it for the innumerable anxiety-related problems our staff dealt with daily.

DAP also comes in spray form and a plug-in, comparable to an air freshener, releasing the pheromone into the air at a constant rate for a set time. A similar pheromone product helps to calm cats with anxiety issues that manifest as inappropriate urination, defecation, or marking behavior. This particular cat pheromone has a message which is supposed to inform the cat that a certain space is "okay" or "safe." We have one of the feline plug-in diffusers turned on in our cat exam room at all times. Studies have shown it can help calm down an unhappy cat. Our staff will often use it to spray an animal's pet carrier right before they go home, and my staff will routinely spray their lab coats and smocks at the beginning of the day with either the dog or cat product, depending on what species they are going to be working with that day.

There have been wonderful advances in anxiety treatment and lower stress handling techniques for animals, but that has not always been the case for as long as I have been practicing veterinary medicine. I remember my first exposure to an aggressive animal was during high school, when I first started working for Dr. Schmelzer. He was my first mentor and the original owner of the practice I would eventually purchase from him. We were in the exam room with a client who'd brought in his very handsome German Shepherd. As Dr. Schmelzer was questioning the owner about the nature of their visit that day, I casually reached down and started stroking the dog's head. The owner noticed and casually commented how this was extremely odd, as the dog usually wouldn't let anyone pet him. It turns out the dog had previously bitten several people, which would've been convenient to know. I must have forgotten the common rule of slowly backing away from a dangerous animal, as it seemed like my hand, followed by the rest of my body, pulled away with

lightning speed. Later, the German Shephard took exception to a vacci-nation needle in his rear leg, and whipped around, biting Dr. Schmelzer hard on the hand. I think at that point they had to peel me from the ceil-ing, but Dr. Schmelzer calmly reprimanded the dog, wrapped his hand up, and finished his appointment.

The lesson I learned that day must have stayed with me, because soon after taking over the practice I was working on a Great Dane who had injured its rear foot. The dog stood at least four feet tall and was very formidable. The owner assured me that the dog was good-natured, which seemed to be the case as I started my examination at the head and worked my way back toward the foot in question. Suddenly the dog decided that it did not like what I was doing, and out of the corner of my eye I saw the huge head and glaring teeth coming towards my head. Luckily the owner also was aware and he yanked on the dog's collar while at the same time, I jumped backward as fast as I could. The dog's teeth just missed my head, but did catch the tip of one of my fingers. Despite the adrenaline rush, or maybe because of it, I calmly wrapped my finger to slow the flow of blood, finished the appointment, and only then did I go to the ER to receive a few stitches to close the wound. To this day, that is the only time I have been a bitten that required suturing.

Recently we had an unusual day in that most of the dogs were very unhappy and tried to bite me or my staff, or in several instances, all of the above. Muzzles were the choice of the day for almost every dog seen that day, and we quickly ran out of the dog appeasing pheromone; I am not sure if there was enough of the product available anyway to make a difference. Then I started to think that maybe someone had played a dirty trick on me. Maybe they had switched the dog appeasing phero-mone with Dog Pissing Off Pheromone, or maybe with Smells Like Beef Pheromone without my knowledge. All I know is that when I went home that night my dog was still happy to see me, so I knew it wasn't me.

BE LIKE MIKE

I have always felt that continuing education was a very important part of my profession. Medical advances happen so rapidly in the veterinary profession, that to keep practicing the highest quality medicine and give my patients the best care, I always attended a large number of continuing education (CE) events. In the state of Missouri, it is necessary to obtain 10 hours of CE credit every year to maintain your veterinary license. I routinely averaged 80-90 hours of CE annually. Not that I consider myself smarter than other veterinarians, I just enjoy the opportunities available to stay current and to "recharge my batteries."

I got into the habit of attending the annual American College of Veterinary Internal Medicine Symposium (ACVIM) every year, which has afforded me the opportunity to travel to a number of nice cities out of state and also provided me with the highest quality of CE, in my opinion. The meeting is geared toward specialists, with a slant towards research and the latest developments, some of which may not have been published yet. Of course, general practitioners are welcome to attend and I have long recommended this meeting to my colleagues as the chance to get the latest, most up-to-date information out there.

Going to this meeting every year, I have heard some of the biggest names in veterinary medicine speak, and also met them on numerous occasions. I am not afraid to introduce myself to the speakers, ask them questions, and hope that they may even recognize me the next time. You get to know who is a good speaker and who will teach you something. A speaker may be the most knowledgeable person on the planet about their subject, but if they cannot connect with the audience, that knowledge is not transferred. I came to learn something, not to sleep through your monotone lecture on renal physiology.

The speakers I listened to the most were the giants of veterinary medicine. I am not sure if the current generation has the same respect and awe that I do for the doctors of veterinary medicine that I was able to listen to and learn from. These were the people who wrote the books that I had learned from in school, and to see them in person, and learn from

them live, was an opportunity I relished every year. And to have them recognize me, even just enough to say hello in the hallways, was a thrill I have to admit. It gave me positive feedback to go back and listen and learn even more.

One year the ACVIM was held at Walt Disney World resort in Orlando, FL. I traveled and roomed with a friend of mine, who is a veterinary radiology specialist, and who was speaking at the conference that year. He was invited to the private speakers' party, and since we had both traveled without our spouses, I was able to tag along as his "plus-one." The party was held at one of the exhibits at Epcot Center, and the venue was closed to the general public. The event was a lot of fun with good food, but the best part was rubbing shoulders with all of those great veterinarians.

I was standing shoulder to shoulder and playing video games with the gods of veterinary medicine. Watching Carl Osborne play Steven Ettinger in some stupid children's game, or Michael Garvey talking to Sharon Center over a plate of chicken wings was incredible. I spent more time people-watching than playing games that night. To see these people, who I considered to be some of the smartest in our profession, as real people just enjoying themselves, was an incredible experience. I am not friends with these giants, but I have great respect for them.

At that same meeting I somehow got roped into being a moderator for one of the talks. The person who had signed up to be moderator was a "no show" and they were short-handed and short on time, so I volunteered. The moderator introduces the speaker, and is in control of the room, addressing problems with the audio or video, ensuring the room is comfortable, and making sure the speaker has water, etc. It is a big responsibility and it just so happened that the speaker I was asked to introduce was one of my favorite vets in the world. Not only vastly intelligent, but he also spoke to everyone in the audience in a way that made us comfortable, telling us that he was one of us, the common folk. Everything he talked about had happened to him, and we were all in this together. I always soaked up every word from him.

So, there I was, in a room of over 500 veterinarians, on the elevated

stage, introducing one of my idols. I made it through the introduction, got off the stage to allow him to do his thing, and then walked back towards the rear of the crowded auditorium. I did my duties of estimating the number of attendees on some official form, and making sure the sound and video were adequate, and the room was not too hot or cold, and then stood in the back with my walkie talkie, trying to look, if not feel, important.

It must have worked, because as I was standing there, a gentleman walked in. He stood near me, surveying the room. He looked at some paperwork in his arms, and I could tell he was lost. It did not appear to me that he was looking for a seat, as there were still open seats in plain view. Finally, he must have noticed me, standing there with my walkie talkie, looking very important, and spoke to me in a hushed voice. He said quietly, "Are you Dr. Michael Schaer?" I grinned, shook my head to say no, and pointed to the smallish figure with the large persona at the other end of the vast room up on the stage with the audience in his hands. "No," I said. "But I wish I was."

ARE CROSS/BREED BANS LEGAL?

A new owner came into the clinic at Gateway Pet Guardians with her dog. It looked like a typical pit bull, which is a common breed in our area. But on the registration form the client filled out that the dog was a Chinese Pit Bull. We do not have that as an option when entering the client's and pet's information in our computer system, so we listed the dog as a Pit Bull Terrier as we suspected it to be. After the appointment I did what any self-respecting veterinarian would do and Googled "Chinese Pit Bull Terrier." Apparently, it is not a recognized breed, but a mix between a Chinese Shar Pei and a Pit Bull Terrier. Okay, I'm going to ask for a show of hands here. How many of you readers think this is a good idea? I love Pit Bulls, but mixing them with a breed that is less than well-loved by a lot of veterinarians is not something I would want to see coming through the door.

During my on-line search I also ran across a breed called a Japanese Pit Bull. There is a recognized breed called a Tosa Inu, which is commonly referred to as a Japanese Pit Bull. I have never heard of this breed, and my first thoughts when I saw the words Japanese Pit Bull, was that this was a cross between an Akita and a Pit Bull. But in reality, it is a breed that is bred for legalized dog fighting in Japan. If this breed would have walked into my clinic, I think I would have retired immediately.

IT WAS NICE TALKING TO YOU

I've always been impressed by how seriously veterinarians take their continuing education. Every time I go to a conference it is wonderful to see rooms full of colleagues, eager to learn new skills and keep up with the latest changes in our field. Refreshing is a befitting word because I always feel refreshed after coming back from a continuing education conference. During my career I tried to attend one or two major or national meetings a year, as well as our annual state veterinary meeting as I have become involved in our state organization on several levels.

Our state veterinary conference is held every January. Recently, the organizers have been attempting to stimulate more attendance by holding it in various cities throughout Missouri. Traditionally, the state veterinary conference is held in a resort town in central Missouri, located on a very large lake. You may have seen this area made infamous on a recent cable television show. Not a very flattering depiction of the area if you know the show I am referring to. This town is bustling with people during the summer months, but there isn't much to do in the middle of the winter, so you might as well go to the lectures and try to learn. Now, that isn't to say that veterinarians don't know how to have a good time at night, once the lectures are over. Then again, it always amazes me how packed the early morning lectures are even after a night of fun.

One year, a well-known veterinary specialist in internal medicine, specifically gastroenterology, was a key speaker at the conference. The speaker was giving a whole series of lectures for an entire day and a half on his area of expertise. I looked forward to the series of lectures as I had read quite a few of his articles and have purchased several books he had authored. He lived up to his advanced billing, and the lectures were both informative and entertaining. I've always believed that you can be the smartest person in your chosen field of expertise, but if you cannot keep your audience interested and awake, they won't learn anything.

During his series of lectures, the conference organizers made an announcement, asking if one of the attendees would be willing to take our guest speaker to the St. Louis airport. That year, I had traveled to the conference by myself, so I immediately thought that this might be a great opportunity. I'd be driving to St. Louis anyway, so I volunteered for the task. During a break in one of his lectures I introduced myself and let him know that I was going to be his chauffeur to the airport. I joked that I'd show him all of the scenery and sights during our three-hour trip to St. Louis. He assured me he was very grateful and was looking forward to it.

I was quick to volunteer not only because I am such a nice guy, but because I had ulterior motives. How many people get the chance to have someone like this alone in a car for three hours of personal continuing education? We could discuss difficult cases I've come across, I could question him on how he treats certain conditions, and most importantly, I'd have an opportunity to get to know him on a personal level. I have to admit that when it comes to certain veterinarians, I get a bit "starry-eyed" when I think about the level of expertise and notoriety that they have achieved. It would be like driving a Hollywood celebrity around, although the average person wouldn't know this veterinarian from Adam. Come to think of it, he actually does practice in Hollywood.

At the end of the conference on Sunday at noon, it was time to pack up and head to St. Louis. I had been bragging to all of my vet friends about my passenger for the ride home, and most were jealous of me for the reasons I stated above. Anyway, I drove the car around to the front of the resort l and picked up my passenger. I had my mental list of topics and questions all ready to go. The drive from the hotel entrance to the road out of town is long, and wouldn't you know it, we hadn't even made it to the main road, when I looked over to see that his head was slumped over against the window and my prized passenger was sound asleep.

That was about the quietest three hour drive I had ever made. I did not even dare turn on the radio in fear of waking him. Although I was sure grumbling on the inside, I will never tell whether he snored or not.

We made it to the airport in plenty of time for his flight and he thanked me for the ride. When he was getting out of the car, he even had the nerve to say, " It was nice talking to you." I wanted to say, "That's what I was hoping to say." He actually did remember me when I ran into him at a national meeting a few years later. Maybe he absorbed some of the subliminal message I kept repeating during his three-hour nap. "Dr. Ed is now your best friend. He can call you up at any hour and get free advice on any cases."

RING A DING DING

Marie, Nicole's daughter and my future step-daughter, was reading something she had just written. It was very deep, something about the human consciousness, and how everything and nothing were actually the same. Anyway, it was a little deep for my shallow brain and I had a hard time understanding it all. She tried to explain it in more detail and said there was a famous painting called "Pavlov's Cave", which might help explain what she was trying to describe. It depicted people in a cave, lit up from behind, looking at their shadows on the wall of the cave in front of them, contemplating their existence. Or something to that effect. Well, despite the further explanation, I was still lost in the shallow end of the gene pool and also mentioned that I had not heard of that painting. She said she would find it on the internet and show us. She looked it up and then proclaimed that she was wrong, it was called Plato's Cave, and not Pavlov's cave. I said no wonder it did not ring a bell.

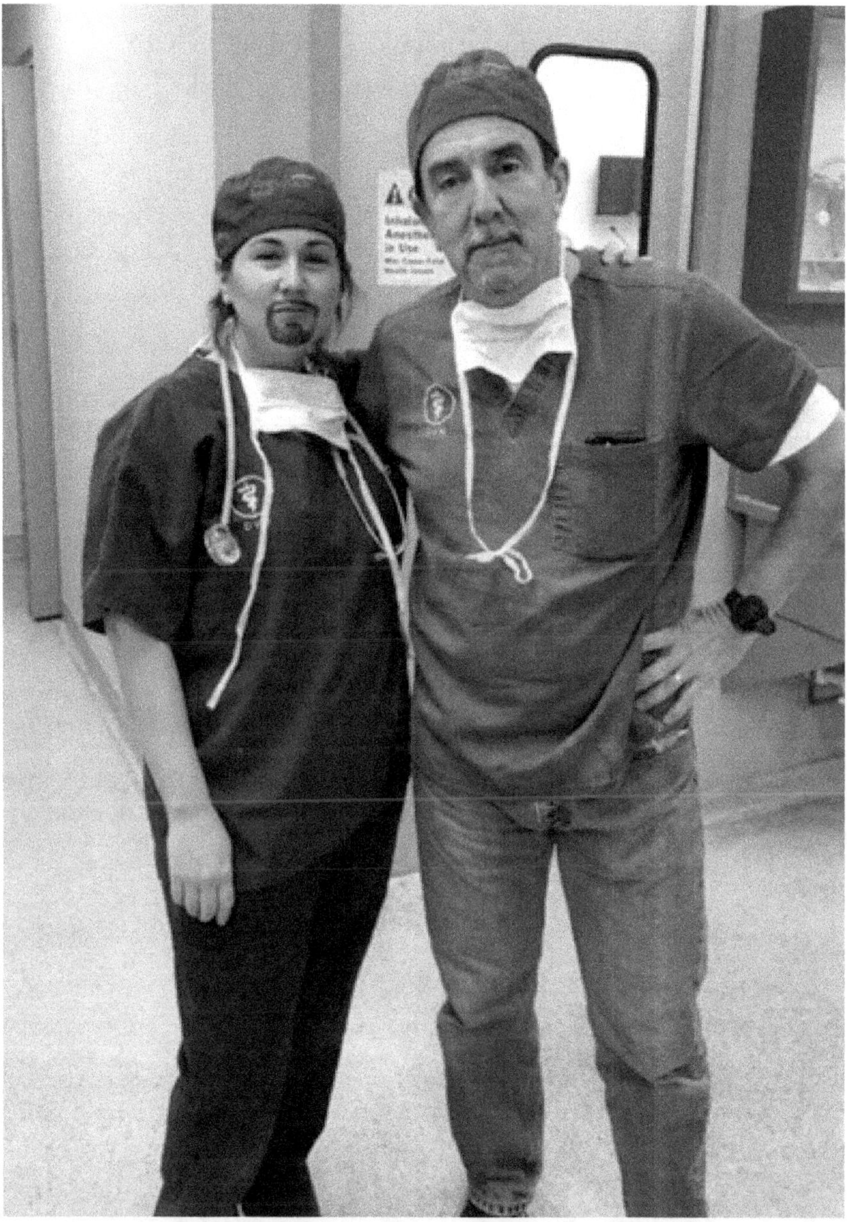

Dr. Ed Look-alike Day at Hillside Animal Hospital

ALL IN THE NAME OF RESEARCH

My former clinic, Hillside Animal Hospital, is located close to both the St. Louis Zoo and Washington University. I was able to do a preceptorship at the St. Louis Zoo, and that, along with our proximity, has cemented a long relationship. We have numerous zoo employees as clients, and have a good working relationship with the zoo veterinary staff. We have been able to help both the zoo and the university with various research projects in the past, providing some behind the scenes assistance, that was nonetheless important to both the projects and to our own sense of importance.

The zoo veterinary team has a reproductive physiology department responsible for the reproductive health of the entire zoo animal collection, but more importantly it is involved with the breeding of rare and endangered species. The zoo staff was working together with the Endangered Wolf Center, a facility located just outside of St. Louis, on a project to understand and help with the breeding of endangered red wolves, possibly the most endangered species of the canine family. A veterinarian from another zoo had developed a non-invasive procedure for uterine biopsies to help determine if any pathology was present prior to breeding the wolves through artificial insemination. Our help was elicited through our client Karen, the leader of the reproductive physiology department at the zoo.

The veterinarian was coming to St. Louis, to teach the biopsy method to other vets involved in reproductive research. We helped the project by providing stray female dogs, which were going to be spayed and adopted out, for the research project. After we initiated anesthesia on an individual dog, the research team would be taught the new procedure for doing uterine biopsies via a rigid scope passed through the cervix. Immediately following the teaching exercise, we proceeded to spay the dogs. Biopsies were taken from the removed uterus by the research team to compare the two methods. The dogs were recovered from anesthesia, and all went on to be adopted into a forever home, and for our efforts the entire staff was invited to a nighttime tour of the wolf sanctuary where we were able

to witness the wolves howling to each other.

Early in my career I was involved in a study of the gorillas at the zoo. Echocardiograms, or ultrasounds of the heart, were being done on the gorillas to establish normal values for that species. At that time, in the late 80s, each animal was anesthetized fully, transported to the zoo veterinary hospital, and kept under general anesthesia while a human cardiologist along with a veterinary radiologist performed the procedure. So, it was a major undertaking. These types of procedures are now done on zoo animals with a "no handling, no anesthesia" approach, but that is what needed to be done at the time.

I was involved peripherally but for a brief moment I felt very useful. A massive male silverback gorilla was under anesthesia on the x-ray table and the procedure was just about to begin when one of the veterinary technicians commented that his pulse oximetry, a measure of how well the blood is being oxygenated, was not where it should be. Everyone else involved was busy so I grabbed a stethoscope and listened to the chest of this incredible animal. I only heard breath sounds on only one side of the huge chest and commented that perhaps the endotracheal tube had been inserted too far and was only inflating that one side. A quick radiograph was taken and the results confirmed my suspicions. The tube was repositioned, the pulse oximetry returned to normal, and the gorilla did great under anesthesia. While my contribution was not a part of the actual research study per se, I did feel good that I happened to be there at that moment to help out in a small way.

Over the years we have dealt with and treated successfully many cases of TVT, or Transmissible Venereal Tumor of dogs. This is a type of tumor that is sexually transmitted as the name implies. While it can be common in certain areas of the world, it was extremely odd that we had such a pocket of cases in this area where I practiced. I had collected bi-opsies and medical information on over a hundred cases, and somehow word about this unusual grouping reached researchers at the prestigious Cambridge University in Great Britain. I was contacted, and my collected information was then forwarded to the researcher for inclusion in two scientific articles published in the *Science* and *Nature* journals. These

studies may someday help human cancer research, but more immediately may prove important in the understanding of the transmissible type of cancer that is decimating the rare Tasmanian Devil population. I was only a small part of a large research study, but my name is included as a contributing author on the manuscripts and I feel very proud of that.

We were also involved in a small study with a researcher from nearby Washington University. We collected testicles from cats that were undergoing neuter surgeries, prior to being adopted into forever homes. I will not begin to understand the nature of the research that involved cat testicles, and was not included as an author on this project, but did get an acknowledgment at the end of the published paper, right before the list of references. It read, "Thanks to Hillside Animal Hospital for providing testicles." Not exactly something to share at a cocktail party.

SLEEP IT OFF

One night, it was very late and I was very sleepy as I was channel surfing, trying to avoid commercials as usual, when I happened upon a commercial for a new drug I had not heard of before. For some reason it caught my attention. The drug was a new sleeping pill made to help you get a good night's sleep. As with any commercial for a pharmaceutical product, it contained a lengthy and boring description of possible side effects of the medication. The narrator droned on and on about "not taking this medication if you are allergic to it." I always wondered how you could possibly know if you are allergic to a brand-new medication that you have never taken before. Then the narrator said, "You should not take this medication if you suffer from narcolepsy". In other words, do not take this sleeping pill if you are prone to fall asleep randomly. At least that is what I thought he said. I was so tired I may have fallen asleep by the end of the commercial.

MUSINGS

SUCKER OR DEDICATED

I recently experienced an episode of déjà vu, with two incidents that happened during my career, separated by over 25 years. I will relate the two stories to you and will show how they are tied together. An elderly client of ours had purchased a Yorkshire Terrier puppy, an impulse purchase at one of those storefront pet shops in the mall. The client brought the puppy in for an examination and vaccinations at the recommended times and things seemed to be going fine with the new addition to her household.

Unfortunately, several weeks into this new relationship, things took a turn for the worse. The puppy got underfoot of the elderly woman, and she tripped and fell after stepping on the little pup. The client was no worse for wear except for some bruising, but the pup suffered a fractured elbow in the mishap.

The client was distraught over this development for a couple of reasons. For one, she, and her children, were worried about the pup causing more accidents and the possibility of a more serious injury to the client. Secondly, the pup's injuries, while not life-threatening, were serious enough that a consultation with a veterinary surgeon was required. Knowing how expensive this would be, the client was faced with the horrible decision that she would not be able to afford the surgery the pup needed. After some frank discussions between us, she relinquished ownership of the pup to the clinic, with the understanding that we would pay for the surgery, and then find the pup a new home.

By now you may have figured out that I ended up adopting the pup. She was renamed Diane, because I already had a male rescue Yorkie named Sam. Don't you wanna go where everyone knows your name? Sorry, brief television interlude. I then made an appointment at the local veterinary specialty clinic for a consultation with the veterinary surgeon. On the day of the appointment, the owner of the practice, Dr. Wayne Hause, listened to my story and started shaking his head and smiling. Then he proceeded to stare at my forehead. I asked him what he was

looking at, and he said he was trying to figure out if it said "dedicated," or just "sucker," across my forehead. You know, at the time I couldn't answer him. Thankfully, Diane made a full recovery and lived a long happy life with Sam and my family.

Fast forward 25 years now during the time of the Covid restrictions. I was doing a Zoom meeting with Dr. Michael Blackwell of the University of Tennessee, interviewing him to be our keynote speaker at our annual state veterinary meeting. If you do not know who he is, you should. He has had a very long, distinguished career, stretching from practice ownership to Dean of the College of Veterinary Medicine at Tennessee, to the FDA Center for Veterinary Medicine, to the Surgeon General's Office. Now he is back at Tennessee in charge of a program called the Center for Pet Health Equity. It is all about trying to ensure that all pet owners, regardless of income or social status, have access to veterinary care for their pets. It is an ideal that is very near and dear to my heart.

Well, our Zoom meeting was going great, and I found Dr. Blackwell to be a very personable and engaging person. He answered all of my questions, and he took a great interest in my current work situation at Gateway Pet Guardians, since we are at the forefront of the movement that he is involved in. As he was listening to me talk about my family, my career, and the path that I have chosen at this stage of my life (when I should be thinking about retirement), I noticed he started to lean forward in his chair and come closer to his computer camera. He smiled, laughed a little, and then proceeded to say that he could not tell if I was dedicated or just a sucker. His words caused that memory of that previous story to rush into my brain. But this time when I heard those same words, I had formulated an answer.

I think there is a fine line in the veterinary profession between being a "sucker" for a worthy cause and being "dedicated" to the alleviation of all animal suffering. When God made me who I am, I have postulated that with the "S" key for sucker, and the "D" key for dedicated being right next to each other on the keyboard, maybe the wrong key got punched somehow. Is there really that big of a difference?

WWJHD?

I am a big fan of T-shirt slogans. As with funny TV commercials and witty memes on the internet, I enjoy really good ones as much as I loathe bad ones. Of course, most T-shirt designs are visual so sharing some examples is challenging. But several slogans do stick out in my mind. For example, I once saw a T-shirt that said:

> Roses are red
>
> Violets are blue
>
> I'm a schizophrenic
>
> And I am too.

Another T-shirt I just loved had two stick figures on the front. One was standing with another stick in its hand. The second figure was just a pile of sticks on the ground. The caption read, "I got your back." I know this has nothing to do with my book, but I am laughing just thinking about it. "Stupid dad T-shirt," I guess. I know my daughters are shaking their heads as they read this.

An associate and I tried once started a T-shirt company. We made up a number of sayings that only veterinarians and veterinary staff would appreciate and tried selling the shirts over the internet and at veterinary conferences. We were mildly successful, but it never took off. One of my favorites was the one that read "I castrate things for a living." It was one of our biggest sellers, especially among fathers with young, dating-age daughters. Another stated "I am your vet, not your therapist," finally, one of the others read

> HBC
>
> BDLD
>
> ADR
>
> Just another day at the office

Only those in the veterinary profession will appreciate the acronyms. HBC stands for Hit by Car, BDLD stands for Big Dog, Little Dog (as in getting in a fight), and ADR (my favorite acronym) stands for Ain't Doing Right. It was fun to sit around and come up with what we hoped would be hot-sellers. Alas, it was not meant to be, and the T-shirt business

ended with little fanfare. Based on the popular "WWJD?" abbreviation for "What Would Jesus Do?", an idea for a shirt slogan which never made it to press was for a shirt that read "WWJHD?" Following is the incident that inspired it.

Gateway Pet Guardians, the animal welfare organization I now work for, is on the forefront of a new wave of animal welfare reform. Our model of community outreach and involvement in our service area is being recognized across the country. One day I was riding around with my good friend Janet, our full time Community Outreach Coordinator. As her title implies, she was the liaison out in the community. She answers all of the phone calls that come into our community hotline, and these requests could involve delivering pet food or supplies to a family experiencing financial difficulty, or a dog house to a family who can keep their dog in the house anymore. Sometimes, it involves making arrangements to get a pet the veterinary care it needed. This outreach was designed to help keep the pets in the home, and from being relinquished to a shelter. I thoroughly enjoyed any time I could spend with Janet doing community outreach. It is very rewarding work which continues today. Now that we have our shelter and the first veterinary clinic ever in East St. Louis, IL, I personally am doing less actual road work, but the mission remains the same.

Among the many stories about my travels with Janet, the one that always stands out happened the summer I had rotator cuff surgery on my shoulder. This involved a long recovery, with six weeks spent in a sling, designed to limit my movement of the delicately repaired shoulder. This also limited my ability to practice veterinary medicine. So, I spent quite a few days riding around with Janet, doing such mundane tasks as delivering flea and tick medication, visiting clients and doing quick exams of their animals on the porch of their houses, trying to determine if the pet needed further medical attention. It was very enjoyable and rewarding work which helped keep my spirits up as I dealt with recovering from my surgery.

It was not unusual for us to get calls about stray animals, and we always investigated them to determine if anything could be done.

Everyone at the shelter knew that if I was riding with Janet, they could expect us to come back with some stray dog, cat, puppy, or kitten in tow. And sometimes we brought in multiple animals. Even though the organization had guidelines in place for the rescue of animals, Janet and I seemed to have an unstated "OK" from the executive director to use our discretion.

One day on our rounds, Janet spotted a rather large Akita walking down the side of the road, dragging a heavy metal chain. He was an imposing figure of a dog, which I was sure had large teeth in that large head of his, and they were probably as large as the two testicles swaying under his tail. Are you getting the idea here? Personally I was not very excited about trying to stop a large male Akita running down the road and trying to determine if I am going to be eaten or licked on the face.

I tried to reason with Janet that this was not a good idea, but she was already out her door and moving towards the front of the car. Not wanting to be labeled as a chicken, I hobbled out of the car to follow her. Remember, at this time I had my right arm in a sling. Well, we made it to about five feet in front of the car, and about ten feet from the dog, when he showed his true colors and let us know which type of Akita he was. He just growled, showed us those large fangs I knew already to be present, and charged us.

You may be familiar with the autonomic nervous system triggering the "Fight or Flight Response." Let me tell you it is very real when a 100-pound Akita is coming at you. Without a word between us or any time to think, Janet and I reversed course and were hightailing back to the car. I guess the dog's instincts were working very well, as he determined in those nanoseconds that with me being in a sling, I was the weaker of the two prey opportunities presented to him that day and he came after me on the passenger side.

This all happened quickly, but I was able to get around the car door which had been left open, thank God, hop into the seat (shotgun!) and pull the door shut with my surgically repaired arm, sling and all. As I said, this was all happening in a matter of seconds, so I did not have time to recall the words of my orthopedic surgeon about not using my arm for any kind of physical activity for a minimum of six weeks. Somehow,

I think if he had been in my situation, he would have told me to use my arm to save my life. I actually felt and heard the dog's jaws snapping at me as the door slammed in his face. Because the dog's attention was on me, Janet was able to get in safely as well and we both sat there catching our breath and letting our heart rates slow down. Meanwhile the dog just turned around and continued down the road, obviously intent on finding some easier prey.

Janet and I had a discussion after that about which stray dogs we would try to help, agreeing on unwritten and unspoken rules about Akitas in particular. As we were riding back to the shelter, in between laughing and crying about our close encounter I thought of the "WW-JHD?" slogan for a shirt which I mentioned earlier. WWJHD?

This stands for "What Would James Herriot Do?" and it is a motto that I have tried to follow during my career. Herriot was a British veterinarian from the 1920s to the 1960s who wrote wonderful stories about his career as a veterinarian. Any veterinarian or veterinary student should know who he is, as I consider his books to be required reading to enter our profession. The stories tell of an early age in veterinary medicine, but the clients, the pets, and the lessons learned are just as applicable today. They are collected in several best-selling books and also formed the basis of the popular "All Creatures Great and Small" TV series.

One involved a large Great Dane which was vomiting, according to the owner. None of the doctors in the practice could get near the dog to perform a physical exam to determine the cause of the vomiting. Dr. Herriot was determined to perform a physical exam and he tried repeatedly to approach the dog. He was met with growls at first, and then outright bite attempts. Finally, his good sense kicked in; he prescribed some anti-vomiting medicine for the dog and hoped for the best. It was obvious that he felt a little defeated by his inability to examine the dog but the reality was just that it was not to be that day.

As I rode in the car, coming down from my adrenaline-fueled high resulting from the near-death experience, I remembered my motto, "What Would James Herriot Do?" I think he would have remembered another old saying among medical professionals. "First, do no harm." Or is it, "First, do not get harmed."

LIVE FROM NEW YORK...

I am not a board-certified veterinary surgeon and do not put myself on
that level, but for a general practitioner I feel like I have the confidence
and ability to take on some cases that others won't. Part of this stems
from my early days in vet school. In didactic block my partner Lisa and
I encountered a diaphragmatic hernia in our first dog spay. The instruc-
tors allowed us to repair the defect before continuing with the surgery. I
believe that day helped establish my confidence.

On one of my free-block rotations I was in Las Vegas working at a private practice. Students were allowed to perform surgery on clients' pets
while under direct supervision of the veterinarian, but not to see clients'
pets during an appointment as they were in other states. I was performing for the first time a cryptorchid neuter on a dog, meaning that one or
both of the testicles has been retained in the abdominal cavity instead of
dropping down into the scrotum. It is important to perform surgery on
these animals, entering the abdominal cavity to remove the retained tes-
ticle(s), as studies have shown that these retained testicles have a higher
propensity to turn into tumors later in life.

As a first-timer, I was a little nervous and I was also a little slow in my
surgical technique. The owner of the practice was a high-strung, type A
personality and demanded precision and time management of his staff.
I was in the middle of the surgery, taking longer to perform this procedure than I do now, when he popped into the surgical room and asked
what the hell was taking so long. I told him to get the hell out of the room
and I would finish when I finished. The staff dropped their jaws and
was amazed that anyone had the nerve to talk to the boss that way, but
apparently it worked, as he and I developed a mutual respect after that. I
did learn a lot at that practice and gained more confidence in my surgical
skills. Oh, and by the way, the boss offered me a job after graduation if I
were willing to move to Las Vegas. How about that?

Fast forward 30 or so years and I am the owner of my own practice
in St. Louis. I have not forgotten those early lessons as I have mentored
many young veterinary students or new practitioners. I always try to

instill confidence in their abilities in the same way it was afforded to me. Having the confidence and ability to perform different and more challenging surgeries makes practice more fun and makes my job more interesting in the long run.

A friend of mine named Shannon was a veterinarian working at the Animal Protective Association (APA). They were asked to be involved in a science symposium for high school students at the St. Louis Science Center. They had this crazy idea to perform a spay surgery on a dog in front of a live audience. Shannon is a good vet but did not perform much surgery, so she asked me if my staff and I would consider this daunting task. After some deep discussion and careful consideration, we did agree. I brought two veterinary technicians and my associate as backup for this undertaking.

Shannon's job was to find the perfect-sized dog, a 40 lb. female mixed breed dog. My staff and I transported our anesthetic machine and oxygen along with surgical light, surgical equipment, and all necessary supplies to the Science Center on the appointed day. We set up on the stage of a large auditorium, with cameras above my surgical field, as well as all around the table, all showing several views of the surgery on large screens for the audience. I had a microphone to explain the procedure in detail as I performed the operation. We all talked to the students prior to administering the premedication sedation to the dog on stage. I then went off stage for a few minutes to an area set up so I could "scrub up," while my staff continued to prep the dog for surgery.

I walked back into the auditorium gowned and gloved in my surgical garb and proceeded to perform a spay surgery in front of a live audience of 200 high school students and teachers. Apparently, I did lose one member of the audience who had to leave the auditorium at the sight of blood, but I guess that's a normal reaction for some people. This surgical demonstration was also broadcast live over the internet to an even larger audience. The video is still out there on the Web if you care to try and find it, and it probably has tens of views by now. The surgery went off without a hitch, and we stayed on stage talking to the students and answering questions, while the dog was recovering from anesthesia.

Overall, it was a great experience, but I am not sure I will ever repeat it. I was nervous of course, but also confident enough to pull it off. When I tell colleagues, they look at me like I am crazy for doing such a thing. It can be difficult to explain to others why I would do such an undertaking. I catch myself saying that I "performed a live spay surgery" in front of an audience, then I have to correct myself to say that I performed a spay surgery in front of a live audience. I sure hope it was a live spay: otherwise, it would have been a necropsy despite the live audience.

YOU SPIN ME AROUND AND AROUND

I have this theory that the earth must spin slower on its axis during the winter months. I know, I know that this theory does not take into account the other half of the world which is experiencing summer at the same time. Just bear with me please. I believe that the world spins slower during the winter time due to all of the pets who gain weight during that season. Every time I examine a pet and explain to the owners that I believe they are "over their ideal weight" (I never say fat), the owners claim that it is just due to being less active in the winter. They promise their beloved pets will lose that "winter weight" very quickly once it warms up. I have not mentioned that a lot of people also make that same claim about weight gain. Perhaps if we take into account the pets and people and their respective winter weight gain, there might be something to this theory. But then again, the world probably starts regaining speed on Jan. 1, as soon as the gyms open in the new year.

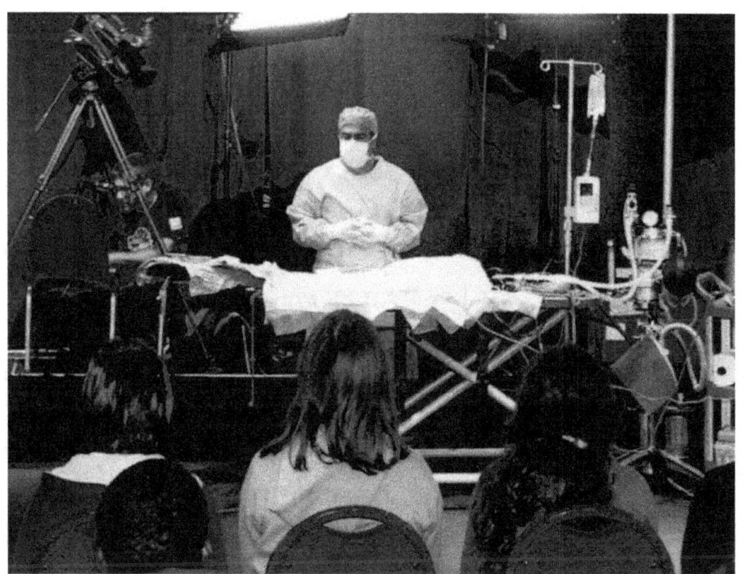

Performing a spay in front of a live studio audience,
and live on the Web, at the St. Louis Science Center

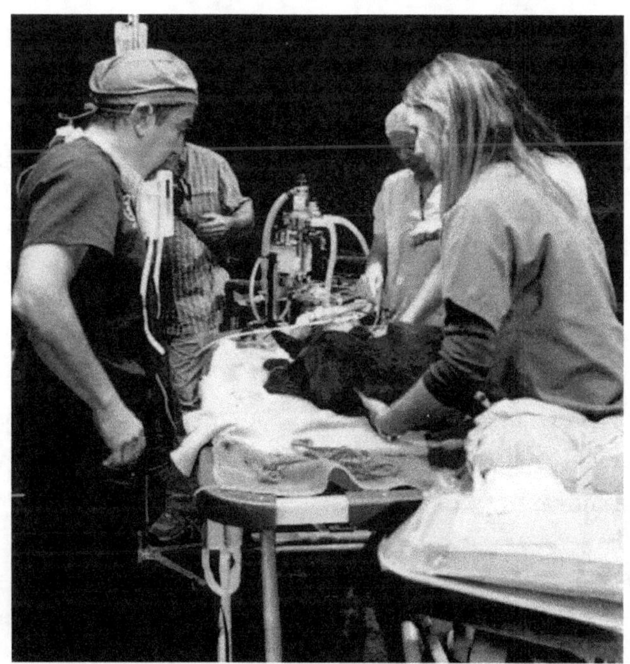

IT'S ALL IN YOUR MIND

I once went to a conference and the speaker was droning on about whatever topic he happened to be speaking about. To be honest, it was the last hour of the last morning of a long weekend and I was having trouble paying attention to the speaker. I am convinced that the speaker was very knowledgeable about the subject he was speaking on, but it was just that I was a little tired, maybe a little hung over, and already heading home in my mind. But then he said something which caught my attention, made me open my droopy eyes, and sit upright in my chair.

During the course of his lecture, the speaker would occasionally cite a study or reference a journal article to support whatever point he was trying to make. Sometimes I am amazed at a speaker's ability to remember some obscure journal article which they probably skimmed over several years ago. No, I take that back. They probably read it from cover to cover, and it is more likely that I skimmed over it, if I even saw it at all. Anyway, this particular speaker referenced a study that had been published in the Journal of Psychosomatic Medicine. So, I asked myself if there could possibly be such a medical journal.

I think that the last time I was in my physician's office for my semi-annual malaria test/CT scan/total body MRI/PET scan/lab work/ prostate exam/cardiac catheterization/colonoscopy, I noticed a copy sitting on the desk. I started to wonder how large the readership of this particular journal really was. Do other physicians or psychologists, besides those who treat hypochondriacs like me, subscribe to it? Or maybe they just think that they do. That must be it. Every month you think that your copy of this month's journal comes, but it really doesn't. You really believe that you have read it from cover to cover, but you really haven't. And you are never the wiser. But you think that you are. You are treating imagined illnesses anyway. Saves a lot of paper.

THE NEW MATH

At work one of the staff mentioned to me that the scale we used to weigh animals on was broken. It was off by at least 12 lbs. they said. The staff member mentioned that they had weighed a patient for surgery to determine the correct dosages for the anesthetic agents and the scale measured the dog as weighing 10 lbs. Apparently, several of the staff thought it was obvious that the dog weighed more than 10 lbs. so they weighed it on the other scale we have and the dog weighed in at 22 lbs. I think I will stop there and let all you readers try to figure out how I knew the first scale was not broken after all.

THE VETERINARIAN WHO CRIED WOLF

When I am working on a crossword puzzle, I have this nervous habit of clicking the button on a retractable pen on and off as I am thinking about an answer. I have been told that I also click the pen on and off against my front teeth, but this is something that I am not aware of. I also absentmindedly click the buttons on the side of my phone as I am walking around. I am not sure if it is a habit or a nervous tic as I am thinking about something else, but one day it almost got me into trouble.

I was leaving my work at Gateway Pet Guardians, located right across the river from St. Louis. I guess I was clicking on the phone while I was walking to my car, which again, is not something I do consciously. Somehow, I clicked the right sequence of buttons and activated the emergency SOS feature on my phone. I had just started the car, and realized that my Bluetooth phone was ringing through the car stereo, which caught me by surprise as I did not realize that I had done anything.

The emergency SOS feature automatically dials 911, and the next thing I knew I was talking to an emergency services operator asking me if I was okay and if I needed emergency assistance. I don't think I was thinking clearly yet about why 911 had been dialed, but I assured the operator that I was just fine and that the call must have been a mistake. Normally the operator is trained to send a unit to my location to make sure, but I guess I was convincing enough and was allowed to hang up and proceed on my way home.

The other feature of the emergency SOS is that your phone sends a text to everyone in your contact list who is identified as an emergency contact, with a small map of where the call was initiated, and a message stating that you are in need of help. I always thought designating someone as an emergency contact was in case someone found your phone, or found you unconscious, they would know whom to call. Boy, was I wrong.

My youngest daughter Nina was the first to call me. She immediately dialed my number and when I answered she asked if I was okay. She told me about the text, showing me on the highway in East St. Louis, and said she did not know if I was in a ditch or had a heart attack. I assured her

that I was fine and apparently had butt-dialed my emergency contact list. I am sure others have done this at some point, but to activate the emergency contact feature you have to press and hold the buttons on both sides of your phone at the same time, and then swipe the emergency SOS button to the right. I am beginning to think that I may need some Ritalin.

My emergency contact list consists of my fiance´e Nicole, my three daughters, my best friend Mark, and my older sister Chris. Would you believe Nina was the only one who called me immediately after getting the text? I did tell her how sorry I was, but also how much I loved her for responding so fast. My sister texted me a few hours later asking if I was okay, and then my friend Mark called a little after that. That left two daughters and one fiance´e who did not respond to the texts. This started me thinking that maybe I was guilty of too many butt-dials. I can understand ignoring a butt-dial, or getting perturbed by too many, but to ignore an emergency text? If I had been on the receiving end of such a text, I would be going crazy until I knew that the person was okay. But that's just me. I sure hope I apologized enough to everyone so that they will not ignore me the next time. Let's hope there is no next time though.

HAKUNA MATATA

One of the veterinary drug distributors we dealt with on a daily basis announced that they were having a contest. They wanted to highlight the circle of life, or something to that effect. They were looking for pictures or slogans that could be used in the campaign, and if you submitted a picture or slogan and it was picked for the campaign you could win some cool prizes. I suggested "SOYLENT GREEN IS DOG!" I have not heard yet if I won anything.

MUSINGS

ANIMAL STORIES

CATCH ME IF YOU CAN

The day was off to a fairly busy start with the usual number of phone-in emergencies when my receptionist, who is also my mother, told me that Sister Pat from the local grade school was on the phone. I took the call immediately. When a nun is on the phone, you take the call.

Sister Pat asked if I could come over right away to catch a peacock that was on the front lawn of the school. "Excuse me," I said? Upon further questioning, Sister Pat assured me that she was not in the habit (no pun intended) of making prank phone calls, and that there was indeed a peacock on the front lawn of the school. He was strutting around displaying his handsome tail feathers and causing quite a disturbance among the schoolchildren. Could I come over right away and catch the bird?

Well, I could come over right away. Whether I'd be able to catch the bird remained to be discovered. Fortunately, I was able to borrow one of my client's big fishing nets I'd used before to catch sick and injured ducks from various city parks. I was ready for the Big Game Hunt.

When I pulled up to the school, I was not prepared for what awaited me. Sister Pat and a flock of schoolchildren were gathered out in front of the school, eagerly waiting for me to save the day. There was also a workman at the school, anxious to see what my plan of action was, appearing to be in no hurry to get back to work.

So, with a large crowd of onlookers following my every move, I tried to catch the peacock. With each futile swing of my net, he took off flying to the top of the small shotgun houses across the street. Shotgun houses are small, narrow houses built with all the rooms in a row from front to back. It is said that if you shoot a shotgun through the front door, it would go out the back door without hitting anything in the house. It was a common type of house in our neighborhood. With every screech he made, I was sure the peacock must have been laughing at me and thoroughly enjoying himself. The game was on. I would swing, he would fly away, wait about ten or fifteen minutes, and then fly back down to the lawn. Needless to say, the crowd thinned rapidly as they discovered I wasn't the Big Game Hunter they were expecting. This game of futile

swings and misses and flying away went on for close to an hour. Even the worker finally gave up and drove away.

Then, my luck changed. The bird flew down and went behind some bushes next to the school. I slowly crept up close to the base of the bush, determinedly Army crawling across the grass. Channeling my best Marlin Perkins imitation, or should I say Jim Fowler, I stealthily crawled a few inches at a time. My breathing slowed and my heart rate and blood pressure lowered lest he sense my presence. Wait, who am I kidding? I did crawl and get dirty but it only took me a few seconds to get close to the bush in question. When I was just on the other side of the bush, the peacock spied me and inevitably started to take off. I took my big net, swept it over my head towards the bird, and I CAUGHT IT.

Triumphant, embodying the Big Game Hunter spirit I knew I had in me all along, I stood up, turned around, and realized there wasn't a single soul to share my victory over the wild beast. My veterinary training did kick in and I remembered how easily birds can get stressed. So, I carefully unwrapped the peacock from the netting and wrapped a large towel around him. What about how stressed veterinarians can get? Adding insult to injury, when I stood up with the bird, he defecated all down my pants leg. Feeling slightly deflated, I pressed the school intercom and told Sister Pat that I had the bird. She said, "Bless you" or something equally holy. I let her know I'd send a bill for the dry cleaning.

With the bird wrapped up in a towel on my backseat, I called my friends at the local zoo. "Were you missing a peacock from your collection?" They assured me they were not missing any birds. They had been receiving a large number of phone calls in the previous four weeks about this particular bird as he made his way across the metropolitan area. Every time, they checked their collection and all birds were accounted for.

"Would you be willing to take in the bird if someone were smart and brave enough to catch it?" I said. When the curator of the bird house stopped laughing, he said of course the zoo would accept the bird and add it to their collection.

"Good," I said, "Because the Big Game Hunter is here at your front gate with his catch."

DÉJÀ VOMIT

It was a typical day at work with the usual amount of emergencies interspersed into our already busy schedule. We seemed to be handling the chaos in an organized fashion, but then my dog, Jack, threw a wrench into our day, making us stop and once again say, "I've never seen that before."

Jack is a Springer Spaniel/Beagle mix rescue dog. He is one of those lucky dogs who is allowed to go to work every day with his owner. He spends most of the day sleeping in my office but will occasionally venture out to see what's happening. It had been such a busy day I really hadn't spent much time in my office at all. So at the end of the day when entered my office, I was met with an unpleasant surprise.

In the middle of the floor, was a very large pile of something unrecognizable. To be honest, at first, I did not know from which end of my dog it had come. I knew it had to be from Jack since he was alone, but I wasn't sure if it was vomit or feces. The color of the pile was brown, there was some apparent mucus associated with it, and there appeared to be some foreign material mixed throughout. But, what really gave it away was the smell.

No, it's not what you think. This pile of unknown origin did not smell as bad as you imagine it would have. As a matter of fact, I detected a faint aroma that reminded me of Easter morning. On closer inspection, the foreign material in the pile of brown was actually wrappers from candy bars. Ah, the mystery was starting to unravel, or unwrap in my mind. It seems that a little while earlier in the day one of our clients discovered that her dog had gotten into the pantry and eaten a whole bag of those small chocolate bars. The client found the empty plastic bag that had at one time contained about 24 miniature chocolate bars. The dog didn't look bad, but the client was aware that chocolate can be toxic for pets. She called us and we had her bring the dog right over.

The patient was showing no ill effects from the ingestion of the chocolate, but the amount ingested was close to a toxic level. Taking no chances, we decided to induce vomiting. We administered hydrogen

peroxide via a stomach tube and walked the dog outside. The dog looked a little nauseous after that, but it actually took a couple of administrations of the peroxide before the dog vomited up a large pile of chocolate, wrappers, and foam on the ground. We performed the standard aftercare, including the administration of activated charcoal to prevent the absorption of any of the chocolate which had not been vomited. We are thankful to say that the patient suffered no problems afterward.

Apparently, Jack noticed all the comings and goings out the side door of the clinic, which is right next to my office, so he decided to follow and investigate. No one noticed that he slipped out after the successful induction of vomiting. He must have thought he was in heaven when he saw that warm meal on the ground waiting for him. But I guess there was enough peroxide still mixed in, because it caused him to vomit soon afterward.

There are a couple of points to be taken from this story. First, my dog Jack is a very slow learner. Later that evening at home we left a couple of brownies, wrapped in foil, unguarded and he helped himself to more chocolate. I calculated that it was nowhere near a toxic dose, so I let him be. No dog needs to be forced to vomit twice in a few hours. Secondly, the original patient in question was indeed a Labrador retriever. I know the obvious question is, "Was it a Chocolate Lab?"

DOG BITES MAIL

We all know the scenario: a mail carrier incurs the wrath of a neighborhood watchdog. It's a very important business, for both the dog and mail carrier alike. Every time a mail carrier heads out to deliver the mail, they run the risk of being bitten by a dog. I in no way want to belittle the perils they can face in doing such an important job. Some will even carry mace or pepper spray to protect themselves. Yes, this can be a dangerous job and everyone should appreciate the mail force for their hard work... but, are you aware that dogs can be at risk by biting the mail? Yes, you heard me right. Not from biting a mail carrier, but by biting the mail.

Instead of mailboxes in front of a house, a lot of houses have mail slots on their front door. Many owners have told me that their dogs go exceptionally crazy any time a mail carrier slides mail through their mail slot. In a lot of cases, the dogs will tear up the mail, which I assume is an act of misdirected aggression. From the mail carrier that triggered it, to the mail itself. I mean, it even smells like the mail carrier!

Once, a client brought their dog in with a peculiar complaint. The check-in form it stated their dog had bitten the mail and now couldn't open its mouth. In the heat of the moment, I didn't read it correctly and thought it was another case of a dog biting a mail carrier. I questioned

the client and she told me that, no, it was just as they had written. The dog had bitten the mail and now could not open its mouth. It seems every day, Pepper would attack the mail as it came through the slot. When the owner arrived home today, she found the remains of a new catalog on the floor. She found her dog sitting on the kitchen floor breathing out the sides of her mouth, and blowing bubbles out between her lips. The dog wasn't having too much difficulty breathing, but the owner did notice that the dog couldn't seem to open her mouth.

The owner rushed Pepper over to the clinic so I could thoroughly examine her. The dog wasn't in pain, but when I lifted her lips, I noticed that her jaws were clenched together. I gently tried to open her mouth, but it wouldn't budge. Once, I'd seen a case of a dog who had dislocated its jaw by biting onto something. I thought that might have been the case for Pepper. I explained to the owner that I wanted to give Pepper a slight sedative to relax her jaws. This way, I'd have better luck trying to pry them open.

We took Pepper to the treatment room and I gave her a sedative. She relaxed and I was able to get a better look at her mouth. I could see some white material sticking out between the incisors at the front of her mouth. I took a hemostat and carefully used it to pry between the jaws. The white material appeared to be acting like an adhesive, so I tried to break the suction between the upper and lower jaws. I was very careful not to break the jaws, teeth, or cause any damage. With some difficulty, the jaws eventually came apart.

The white material turned out to be paper from the torn-apart catalog. Apparently, in taking a big bite out of the catalog and tearing it into pieces, the paper became macerated and wedged in the front teeth, and it was thick enough and wet enough to lock them together. Pepper recovered very quickly from her mild sedation, with no damage to her mouth at all. She lived to attack the mail again. Or maybe she learned her lesson that sometimes the mail bites back.

I've heard of cases where dogs bit the mail carrier, but this was the first case of the mail ever biting back. I like to think mail carriers everywhere gave a reserved cheer at the irony of it all.

POLLY WANT A .45?

While still practicing in my old clinic building, I received a phone call in the middle of the night. As a veterinarian, a call in the middle of the night could mean anything from a frantic client with a blocked tom cat who cannot urinate, to a nervous owner with a new puppy who has developed diarrhea. I never got used to being awakened by the jolting ring of our phone. Nowadays of course, I rely on my cell phone. But the dreaded feeling of being hurled out of a deep sleep will always be the worst in the world.

But could it possibly be worse when the Police Department is on the other end of the phone? I was still climbing out of my deep slumber, and from what I could tell, an officer on patrol had driven by my clinic and saw the side door open. He called the dispatcher, who had then called to request my assistance on the scene. Needless to say, the thought that my clinic had been broken into made my heart sink.

When I reached the clinic, I pulled around to the side of the building and found what appeared to be a fairly relaxed police officer leaning on the hood of his car with his arms crossed. I quickly got out of my car and introduced myself. He did the same, and immediately started laughing. Not seeing the humor in the situation, I nervously asked the officer what was so funny.

He asked me, "How much do you like your bird?" I must have still been a little foggy from being abruptly awoken, because I couldn't figure out what he could possibly be referring to. He informed me that everything was okay and that I'd see what he meant in a second. After we entered the building, it became crystal clear.

It just so happened, I'd boarded a large macaw at the clinic for a client. It was one of those very beautiful, blue and yellow macaws who live a long time. The bird had also acquired quite the vocabulary during its life. The client had brought the macaw to the clinic in a large wrought iron cage. The only place we could keep it was in the vestibule, right near the side door of the clinic.

I could just imagine the scene. The officer, probably a rookie on his first solo tour of duty, was driving by and spotting the clinic door open. He calls it in, and then decides to investigate for himself. With his gun drawn, he slowly enters the darkened clinic and identifies himself. Then, someone or something in the dark says, "Hello!" The officer, high on adrenaline, wheels around, ready to empty his gun into the darkened space towards the mysterious voice. I am sure it took several minutes for his heart to stop pounding.

How in the world would I have explained that to the macaw's owner? "I am so sorry to inform you that your bird was killed during the course of a break-in at the clinic. Not by the perpetrator, but by one of our city's finest. These few feathers are all that is left." As it was, I already had a hard enough time explaining some new cuss words the bird picked up during its time being boarded.

By the way, I did lose a few dollars out of the cash drawer in the break-in. Nothing else of value was gone. But I can only hope that the perpetrator was just as scared as the police officer had been when he first entered the building. I can only assume he was, otherwise he may have realized the few measly dollars he got in the break-in were no way near what the macaw and his cage were worth on the black market.

BULLDOG BOOGIE NIGHTS

In 1995 a movie called *Boogie Nights* starring Mark Wahlberg was released. This film was about the porn industry and Mark played a character whose stage name was Dirk Diggler. *Boogie Nights* was about the porn industry without being a full-fledged porn movie. Now, you can use your imagination since I'm unable to describe the full movie in detail, but to be the star attraction in a porn movie you must be, how do I say this, well endowed.

We had a patient at our animal hospital who seemed hell-bent on trying out for the canine version of *Boogie Nights* every time he stepped foot into our clinic. Norman was an English Bulldog and along with that breed came all of the traits that we veterinarians associate with it. Norman was overweight, snorted often, breathed as if he was gasping for his last breath, and had a face that only his mother could love.

Besides the usual problems almost any Bulldog would have, Norman had a particular problem, or affectation, if you will, that made him especially interesting. Norman was quite oversexed and tended to get aroused whenever any female staff members were present. He'd usually start to get an erection and then promptly attempt to hump the leg of any nearby human. Now, whenever my technician Matt or I worked on Norman, he'd occasionally start to get aroused, only to quickly realize that the rest of the females in the clinic had somehow retreated to the backroom. After his astute realization, Norman would settle back down. Or should I say, Norman's male appendage would settle back down.

As this isn't the most pleasant visual, it became a part of our normal routine for the female staff members to avoid going anywhere near Norman when he'd waltz in for an appointment. This particular problem surfaced, so to speak, occasionally when his owners took him out in public. One time it was extremely embarrassing for the owners and a little serious for Norman.

Norman and his owners were out at a local park. It was a very nice day and a lot of people were enjoying the sunshine and getting some fresh air. Included were lots of young children. Norman, as usual, started to get a little overstimulated…but the real problem began when Norman started dripping blood from the tip of his penis. What happened was that the mucosa of the urethra prolapsed just out a tiny bit, but enough to cause it to bleed a lot. When I say dripping blood, that is a complete understatement. It was a great deal of blood according to the owners.

I was not there to witness the disturbance in the park, but Norman's owners say that people started to point, stare, and even children were asking what was wrong with the doggie. It was at that point that they started questioning their choice of dog breed. Not wanting to be arrested for animal abuse or indecent exposure, they immediately called me and I met them at the clinic.

I had only seen this problem in dogs once before, but at least I had some experience in how to deal with it. Norman was anesthetized, the bleeding mucosa was sutured back into place and Norman went onto a full recovery. I should mention that this problem surfaced again at a later date which necessitated another small surgery. But this time, I guess I was a little more aggressive with my suturing because his affliction has not recurred.

To help ensure this from happening again, I told Norman's owners that it was really necessary to prevent him from getting overstimulated. Before they realized I was being serious, they had blank stares on their faces. But then they just laughed at me, as if they could contain Norman and his, well, you know.

THE DUKE

Did you know that John Wayne appeared in more than 200 movies? Or that out of those movies he actually died in only 8 of them? Or that he only won an Academy Award once? Well, I sure did know all of those bits of trivia. In fact, one of my favorite trivia questions is to name the 8 films in which The Duke died. He was arguably one of the most loved movie actors to ever grace the silver screen. I have always been a huge fan of his and never miss a John Wayne movie when it comes on. As a matter of fact, when I was 9 years old, my father took me to New York City and while there we saw *True Grit* at Radio City Music Hall. This is one of my most cherished memories of my father and me. By the way, The Duke won his Academy Award for Best Performance by an Actor for that role. The original version blows the remake away in my opinion. I mean come on, that scene when Rooster Cogburn (Wayne) comes riding down the valley with the reins in his mouth and 2 guns blazing, against Ned Pepper (played by Robert Duvall no less) is one of the most classic gun battles in all movies. And then La Boeuf (played by Glen Campbell, yeah that's right) saves The Duke's ass from a thousand yards away with his rifle right before he dies after getting conked in the head with a rock by Tom Chaney. I am starting to get a little teary-eyed thinking about that scene.

I guess you've figured out I am a movie nut. I love movies, movie trivia, and everything about movies. So, this has been a little lengthy introduction to my next story. It obviously revolves around John Wayne and I need to get started to tell you about it. Today one of my long-term clients came in with his new puppy. After practicing veterinary medicine for 30 years at the same practice I have seen quite a few clients through the years with multiple pets. This particular client had lost his dog Wally to cancer a few months before. This was the second dog that Terry has had brought in and we took care of from birth to death. Wally was one of those dogs that just made my job great. He was a beautiful Australian Shepherd, as smart as any dog I have ever met, and as well trained as any I have ever seen. To put it mildly he was just one of our favorite dogs

we have had the pleasure to take care of. I have fond memories of seeing Terry and Wally down at the neighborhood park playing frisbee. They live on the street that I take home from work and it was not unusual to see Wally outside, sitting obediently on the front lawn, while Terry and his wife worked outside. Wally never needed to be on a leash as he was that well trained.

Near the end when Wally got sick my daughter Anna, now a practicing veterinarian working with me at the clinic, saw Wally as a patient. I thought that was very fitting as the torch was just beginning to be passed on to her. Anna did a great job with Wally, and he actually rebounded for a while and felt a lot better. This allowed the family some quality time together. Unfortunately, we did finally find that Wally's illness was too much for him and the decision was made to end his suffering. That day was one of those that sticks with you for a long time. We know that we are making the right decision on the dog's behalf, but it still hurts for us as much as the family. Anna handled the euthanasia but I made it a point to go in afterwards to say goodbye to Wally and give Terry and his wife a hug. I am not afraid to say that I cried that day.

As I said earlier, today Terry came into the clinic with a new puppy. Duke was an 8-week-old Belgian Tervuren. This is a relatively rare breed around our parts, and they are a breed which looks similar to German Shepherds, although they tend to be a little darker in color. They are very good-looking dogs and this puppy was off to a great start in that regard. Duke was a fantastic patient that day and was as relaxed and comfortable in the exam room as any puppy I have ever seen. We found him to be in great health and vaccinated him.

Terry then told me the story about how he came to pick this breed of dog. First of all, he said that he could not bring himself to get another Australian Shepherd as it was still too painful and there could never be another Wally. But what he told me next just made me break out in a big smile. He told me one of his favorite movies was *Big Jake*, starring John Wayne. In the movie Wayne plays a rancher whose grandson is kidnapped. It is up to the Duke, Big Jake McCandles, to rescue the grandson he had never met. His traveling companion on this adventure is a faith-

ful dog named Dog. Dog turns out to be quite the hero, saving Big Jake a couple of times and also helping to save the grandson at the end. Unfortunately, in the movie Dog ends up losing his life to save the boy. Terry told me the dog in the movie was supposed to be a Belgian Tervuren, and that is why he always wanted to get one someday.

That story that Terry told me about the origin of his dog and the name he chose for him really made my day. It encompassed not only my love for dogs, but my love of movies. It also made me do some research about Dog and the movie *Big Jake*. It turns out the dog in the movie was a canine actor named Laddie, who actually was a Collie. They apparently colored his fur to make it appear darker and make him look more like a shepherd (or Belgian Tervuren) in this case. In fact, during the movie there are a couple of times when the coloring had worn off and the dog would all of a sudden appear to be a lighter color. Laddie won a PATSY Award that year for his portrayal of Dog in *Big Jake*. The PATSY (Picture Animal Top Star of the Year) Award is given annually to animal performers by the Hollywood chapter of the American Humane Association.

I am not sure if I will tell Terry about the research I dug up about the breed and particularly about the movie. I don't think it will matter much to him either way. I know it will not lessen how much he already loves Duke, and it certainly won't change how much we enjoy having him and his beloved pets as clients and patients. Besides, I learned some new trivia to impress my friends with.

ACK! HAIRBALL

The rescue organization I work for was invited to bring some cute dogs available for adoption over to a FURRY Convention that was happening in our town. Furries are people who have an interest in anthropomorphic animals, or animals with human qualities. Many furries create their own animal character, known as a fursona, which functions as their avatar within furry communities. In simple words these are people who enjoy dressing up in life size costumes as animals. By no means am I making light of the group by mentioning them in this story. It was just that while Gateway was there with several cute dogs available for adoption, we raised over $7000 in donations. Makes me wonder if we would have raised that much if we had not brought a Chinese Crested Dog and an Xoloitzcuintli.

I CAN'T BELIEVE I ATE THE WHOLE THING

In the animal world, the award for gastronomic feats has to go to the vulture, in my opinion. I know what you are thinking, not the most elegant and deserving of animals. But when you stop and think about what they eat on a daily basis, it just has to blow your mind. I mean really, do they have a sense of smell? Do they not have a gag reflex or is the vomiting center in their brain underdeveloped through evolution to allow them to eat what they do? And how strong must their stomachs be to allow for the dead and putrid material to pass through. I mean, it's just offal. Sorry, brief dad joke interlude there. Seriously, I realize studying vultures would not be an easy scientific venture, but how amazing must the bacterial microbiome of their GI tract be.

A dog or a cat is a different animal, no pun intended. Sometimes they can eat unusual things and suffer no untoward consequences, but other times bad things happen, like diarrhea, vomiting, or obstruction of the GI tract. I have compiled a list of things I have seen a pet eat without causing any real problems.

Dogs and cats under my care have eaten the following items and lived to eat more the next day.

- An entire take-out Chinese dinner off the kitchen table. I advised the owners not to worry but to be ready to feed the dog in an hour as he will be hungry again.

- An entire frozen roast, butcher paper and all.

- An entire antique wooden duck decoy. It looked very real, but I can't imagine it tasted like duck

- A complete BBQ dinner of pork steaks, while still on the grill

However, I have either removed personally or witnessed a wide variety of strange objects, also called foreign bodies in veterinary medicine, that have been removed from the GI tracts of dogs, and occasionally cats.

- An entire baseball, chewed up but recognizable. The dog literally tore the cover off the ball and proceeded to eat the rest of the ball also.

- Women's underwear- I've learned to always be discrete when talking to the spouse, as they may not be the spouse's brand or size.

The same goes for women's pantyhose.

- A total of 21 racquetballs from the stomach of a Golden Retriever.
Don't worry, he bounced right back from surgery.

- An entire can of Coca-Cola, chewed up but still recognizable.
It was the real thing.

- A sales tax mil, which is a coin made of zinc that used to represent a
fraction of a cent for sales tax purposes. The dog was just a small percent
off that day.

- Many other coins of various denominations. Don't nickel and dime me.

- Many fishing lures and hooks. I don't fish, so I won't lie about this.

- Socks, which amazes me as it is never clean socks that the dogs
go after.

- Easter basket grass, a favorite of cats. Maybe they prefer plastic
over paper.

- Rubber bands- I'm not stretching the truth here.

- Many unrecognizable bones

One patient, a big yellow goofy puppy of the Labrador persuasion
named Dodo (it's not her real name, but it should be) came in vomiting
with a greatly distended abdomen. Radiographs revealed a stomach
distended with some kind of unrecognizable material. A gastrotomy was
performed and our team removed five pounds of grass from the dog's
stomach. The operating room smelled like a cow's rumen that day.
Dodo recovered uneventfully, or so we thought.

Lo and behold, she was back at the clinic seven days later vomiting
again. This time, the reason was obvious. Her owners told us that, while
left alone for one day, Dodo had eaten about three square feet of drapery
from their bedroom. Radiographs revealed another distended stomach,
full of fabric, and lead drapery weights. We attempted endoscopic
retrieval but the cloth was too heavy to remove. Another gastrotomy
was performed and she recovered uneventfully. We are still looking
for her brain.

CLIENT STORIES

TEMPERATURE'S NORMAL

I have heard it said many times that veterinarians are considered one of the most honorable and respected professionals by the general public. When you consider the faith put in us by our clients, in entrusting the care of their "family members," it is understandable. But with that trust comes an inherent pressure to perform, basically to not screw up. I personally have felt that pressure on numerous occasions and usually welcome it as I consider it the result of the faith the clients have in our ability and compassion. But occasionally there has been a situation where I thought I had lost that trust, or potentially could lose that trust. After being put on a pedestal, I thought this case might be the one to finally knock me off.

Mrs. Marzetti, a very nice little old lady from The Hill neighborhood, was one of our best clients. She called urgently one morning and was extremely distraught. Sophie, her beloved toy poodle, just had a "stroke." Stroke is a word that veterinarians hear a lot. Owners almost always believe any given diagnosis, just so they're able to rationalize what's wrong with their pets, and will search far and wide on the internet for help. It seems when Sophie woke up in the morning, she wasn't able to properly walk. She was repeatedly falling over to one side and was even curling her body up to the same side. We could tell how upset Mrs. Marzetti was, so we told her to come right over.

When clients call us with a sick pet, it's our policy to see them as quickly as possible, no matter how busy we are. We try to empathize with how upsetting a pet's illness or injury can be to the owner, much less the pet.

When Sophie was examined, she was just as Mrs. Marzetti described her. She kept falling over to her left side and was unable to stand up unassisted. When lying down, she'd curl her body to the left into a tight ball. Closer examination revealed that she also had nystagmus, a rapid movement of the eyes associated with disturbances of the sense of balance. During the course of my examination of Sophie, I inserted my new digital thermometer to assess her body temperature.

Sophie's physical examination findings were typical for a condition called Idiopathic Canine Vestibular Syndrome. In simple terms, the condition is caused by an inflammation of one of the cranial nerves, the one which controls our sense of balance. In dogs, this is a fairly common syndrome we see, and there is usually a very sudden onset. A dog will be perfectly normal one day, only to wake up the next day like Sophie, unable to walk and suffering from vertigo.

I tried very carefully to explain all this information to Mrs. Marzetti. The most important part of my explanation was that this condition was self-limiting, and in a few days, Sophie should be completely back to normal. Since she was such a small thing, it wouldn't be any trouble to care for her. I advised her to keep Sophie on the couch, carry her every-where, hand feed her if necessary, and in a few days, she should be as good as new.

Mrs. Marzetti seemed to be appeased with my explanation. Calming her was just as important as finding out was wrong with her beloved dog. Sometimes the most important thing we dispense out of our hospital is peace of mind. She seemed happy when she left and I promised to check in on her and Sophie in a few days to make sure they were both doing okay. She left carrying Sophie in her arms, a place I figured the poodle would be spending a lot of time during the next few days.

The day continued as usual, while we prepared to see our next ap-pointment. The next client and patient of the day were led into the exam room, and a very cute little puppy was placed on the exam table for its initial visit. After talking with the client about where the puppy was from, what food they were feeding it, and if it had received any vaccina-tions as of yet, I proceeded to examine the pet. But as I reached for my new digital thermometer, I realized it wasn't on the counter in its usual holder. I looked all over, including the floor, but it was nowhere to be found. About this time I had this sinking feeling that I knew where the thermometer was. But first, I had to finish this appointment.

After I was finished with this appointment, I told my staff that I had to go out for a few minutes. They looked at me and shook their heads, as it was not quite lunch time. I didn't explain myself any further, as I was a

little embarrassed about where I was going.

I hopped into my car and drove a few blocks over to Mrs. Marzetti's, a nice little bungalow on a quiet street in my own neighborhood. Luckily, it was the middle of the day, there was no traffic, and she lived very close. Hesitantly, I rang her doorbell. When she answered her door, I spotted Sophie over her shoulder, curled up in a ball on the sofa on a soft pillow, with the television on, probably tuned into Animal Planet. It's always wonderful when clients follow my instructions to the letter. Mrs. Marzetti had a very puzzled look on her face. From that point on my hesitancy ended. I just said "Excuse me" and promptly pushed past her.

As I walked into the very neatly appointed living room, I could see that the television I had heard was actually tuned into Jeopardy. As I walked confidently and swiftly over to the sofa, I imagined I could hear Alex Trebek saying, "The answer is 101.5 degrees." I continued over the sofa, carefully pulled the nice warm afghan from around Sophie, pulled my new digital thermometer out of Sophie's rear end, glanced at it, and then made a big show of putting it into its plastic container and into my front pocket of my shirt. I then tucked Sophie back into her nice little bundle and gave her a pat on the head.

I then left just as I came in, but not without saying just two little words to Mrs. Marzetti. As I got into my car and drove away, I could see her in my rear view mirror smiling and shaking her head. I knew then that while this Weeble may have wobbled, he had not fallen off of the pedestal. What two words did I speak to Mrs. Marzetti as I left the house? Well, the only two words I could think of to save my dignity. "Temperature's normal."

MUSIC TO MY EARS

The annual wellness exam for the older Border Collie began just like any other routine checkup. The dog was in good physical condition and wasn't experiencing any specific problems. I made sure to go over the physical exam findings and explain the results of the annual heartworm and fecal tests. Naturally, at the end of every appointment, I ask the client if they have any other questions. The client leaned towards me, spoke very quietly, and said he had an unusual question.

After 20 years of practice, I thought I'd heard it all. So, nothing could have prepared me for what this client was about to ask. Without missing a beat, the gentleman asked if I'd ever heard music playing from a dog before. At this point, my technician quietly excused herself to share this information with the rest of the staff. While maintaining a serious and cool demeanor, I asked the client to explain exactly what he meant.

Quite seriously, the client said that he heard music playing whenever his Border Collie stretched out in a certain position. According to him, the music only lasted for 10-12 seconds and sounded clear as day. He even told me that on multiple occasions, he heard a particular song play-ing. I wasn't prepared when the client told me this particular song was "Mary Had a Little Lamb." I was trying extremely hard to maintain my cool demeanor and not smile or make the client feel badly. I really had no suggestions as to what could be causing what he was hearing. Finally, I guess after some uncomfortable silence, he asked if his dog's identifica-tion microchip could act as a receiver or transmitter.

It was at this point that I expected Allen Funt to come running out and announce I was on *Candid Camera*. Or, to make myself sound less old, I expected Ashton Kutcher to pop up from behind the operation table and yell, "You've been punked!" While I was barely able to contain myself, the client maintained total seriousness, Even though I calmly addressed the owner's question, I couldn't help but go off on a thoughtful tangent.

I'm a trivia nut who likes old TV and movies a lot. The owner's question got me thinking about an episode of *Gilligan's Island* where Gilligan gets knocked in the head, and all of a sudden, the fillings in his teeth start acting like a radio receiver. It was strange, but fortuitous, since the castaways' radio had stopped working just before Gilligan's accident. The castaways were able to hear information about an incoming storm, which in turn saved their lives. But alas, the radio in Gilligan's head went away when he was smacked in the head again.

I think it was the Skipper who smacked Gilligan in the head and made the radio signals go away. The Skipper was prone to smack his "Little Buddy" on the head when Gilligan said or did something stupid. Believe me, there have been many times when I wished I could smack a client in the head for saying something stupid. But then again, I guess I'd have fewer clients and less to write about.

I searched my memory and never did come up with an answer to that strange question posed that day. I could not bring myself to post this case on the veterinary forum that is frequented by veterinarians all over the country, asking for ideas. Would my colleagues think that maybe I had gone off the deep end, or would they be understanding and offer some solid suggestions? I guess I was too afraid to find out which it would be. And besides, for reasons not known, the subject was never brought up again by this client on subsequent visits.

And finally, I had to wonder if there was anything to the particular song this dog was supposedly playing inside his body? I mean, if you were a Border Collie, wouldn't you play "Mary Had a Little Lamb" if you could? What else do Border Collies think about all day, but sheep? I guess I would be more impressed if the client had heard Ted Nugent playing "Cat Scratch Fever."

THE CLIENT WE NEVER MET

The staff at City Animal Hospital had never met one of our most infamous clients. We knew of her as Mrs. Brown (as in recluse) and by her pet's names, but she'd never set foot in our clinic. We certainly recognized her voice on the phone, which was a cross between a sultry Bette Davis and a gravelly Anne Ramsey, who is the actress from the movie *Throw Momma from the Train*. Once you got past "Good morning," you never have the chance to get another word in edgewise. From that point on, any poor soul who answered the phone had to listen and pray that an emergency would happen just so they'd have a viable excuse to cut her off.

Mrs. Brown's animals were regulars at our clinic, as they came in for their yearly vaccinations, flea dips, and various ailments. But the pets were always brought in by a succession of young, virile, college males, instead of Mrs. Brown. My female staff would anxiously await these studs as they fulfilled their duty of bringing Mrs. Brown's pets in.

Her pets were boarding at the clinic while Mrs. Brown and her latest student "helper," Chad, were off to Palm Springs for...well, we didn't know exactly why they were going to Palm Springs. My staff and I always had interesting ideas, which were exciting and disgusting at the same time. The day of Mrs. Brown and Chad's expected return came and went, and no one appeared to collect the animals. We phoned Mrs. Brown and she informed us that Chad was responsible for picking up the animals and she would look into the matter, as she was unable to come herself. This same conversation took place for the next five days with no one coming to collect her pets. We were starting to feel sorry for the animals, and just a little bit curious about what was really going on.

Finally, on a Saturday afternoon at closing time, with still no prospect of the animals going home (meaning that they would have to stay until Monday morning at least), I called Mrs. Brown and asked if I could deliver her animals. She seemed almost bothered by the suggestion, but agreed to it anyway. Needless to say, I was very appreciative of the opportunity to finally meet this mysterious client.

When two of my employees overheard, they immediately jumped at the opportunity to go along, under the pretense that I desperately needed their help with the animals. I couldn't recall the last time my staff so eagerly volunteered to stay after hours. They obviously were as curious as I was. As we drove to her apartment, we all discussed what possibly could be awaiting us. I envisioned Greta Garbo, in *Grand Hotel*, sitting in her parlor, not wanting to be disturbed. Boy, was I wrong.

The apartment was elaborately furnished with antiques and several of those paintings that seem to take up half a wall. A visiting nurse opened the door, and upon seeing that we were delivering two dogs and a cat, immediately deposited herself in the hallway, stating that she'd stay there until her relief person came. She wanted nothing to do with the dogs, who would rather lick your face than bite you. I believe the nurse saw a great opportunity to get away and was eager to take it.

With the nurse in the hall and no one to help us, we found ourselves standing in the foyer of this immense apartment calling out to Mrs. Brown. Hearing her speaking to us from the bedroom, we went in search of this mysterious client only to find not Greta Garbo, but Cruella de Vil, older, meaner, and bedridden. Mrs. Brown was propped up in her massive bed by a sea of pillows, with the nightstand at her side brimming with prescription vials of all sizes and an assortment of liquor bottles.

After we picked up our jaws from the floor, we attempted to have a conversation with this woman, but quickly discovered that it was impossible. When my assistant made the comment that her animals were happy to see her, she replied "Of course I'm happy, I'm nearly insane." Needless to say, it was downhill from there. Somehow I was able to help her write a check for the amount she owed us for the boarding. Of course, many jokes were made later about how much I could have written the check for.

My staff wanted to search the closets for the missing Dalmatian puppies. I just wanted to get out of there as soon as possible and get back to my other insane clients.

TOYS WILL BE TOYS

We got a call from a client who was fostering a dog for a rescue group. She said the dog had been vomiting for several hours. We tried to get some more information from her about the dog, but she seemed reluctant to divulge too much information to us. After some coaxing, she told us that she knew the dog had eaten something it shouldn't have. She had our attention, but later we wished she was not quite so forthcoming.

Even though the client had no more difficulty telling us what had happened, I now find it rather embarrassing to retell the story. It seems the client had come home and found that the dog had chewed up and eaten her female personal self-satisfaction device. That was enough information for us. We really wanted the client to just bring the dog in. But she proceeded to tell us what the brand of item it was, what it was made of, what texture, and what color it was. Of course, the story was repeated to everyone in the clinic within a few minutes of the phone being hung up.

The dog was eventually brought in because he continued to vomit, and developed bloody diarrhea. The client vividly described all the pieces of the device that were in the vomitus and the diarrhea. Thankfully, after taking radiographs and examining the dog, we did not think he would be needing surgery. We treated him symptomatically and he did go on to make a full recovery.

The client was very grateful for our efforts. My staff was very grateful for her providing a break in their routine. Despite the rather expensive visit to the vet, she told us she really could not be mad at the dog. "After all," she said, "the dog thought it was just a toy."

CLIENT STORIES

MY BIG FAT GREEK CLIENT

I've heard it said before that eventually, dogs and their owners start to look alike. There are memes all over the internet attesting to this. You may be familiar with the famous picture of a man with very long, flowing, windswept hair driving in a convertible with someone next to him with long, flowing hair. Except that it is an Irish Wolfhound in the seat next to him and not another person. Unfortunately, another "trait" we may share with our best friends is that studies have shown that over 60% of the pets brought into a veterinary clinic are over their ideal body weight. I think this is why I strive to help my pets maintain an ideal body weight.

If there's any truth to either of these facts, then I had two very good reasons to feel sorry for "Tuffy," a cute little mixed breed terrier owned by Mrs. Marina Very Greek. First and foremost, I want to say there's absolutely no doubt in my mind that Marina loves her pets with all of her heart and soul, as well as her kitchen. There is nothing she wouldn't do for them. Unfortunately, there's nothing she wouldn't cook for them either. If her husband is any indication, it was obvious that Marina happens to be a very talented cook.

Marina's husband had been a very large man, but to his credit, dieting has helped him lose a good amount of weight. He still has a way to go before he reaches his "ideal weight." Tuffy, on the other hand, has an even longer way to go before he can even think about reaching his ideal weight. Of course, this is because he eats whatever Marina, and her husband, eats. Sometimes I like to kid around with my clients, telling them there's enough dog there to make two very cute dogs

One of Tuffy's favorites, according to Marina, is Quacker Oats, or as they are more commonly called, Quaker Oats. Marina had a wonderful and endearing way of fracturing the English language with her heavy accent. Tuffy apparently enjoys Mediterranean tastes, for he has been known to sample moussaka, dolmades, and not to be strictly Greek… even spaghetti and meatballs. Marina has even been known to apply some old-fashioned Calamari Lotion to Tuffy's various itchy spots. We, of course, knew she was referring to Calamine lotion. But then again, maybe it really was calamari lotion. What do I know? It's all Greek to me.

Hiking to 14,000 in Peru while visiting Machu Picchu (2018)

WAS IT ROCKY III OR ROCKY IV?

A family consisting of a mom, dad, and young son came into the clinic with their two new puppies. Their son was named Apollo and the two puppies were Drago and Thor. I told them 4 times during the meeting that Thor should have been named Rocky.

MUSINGS

ME AND MRS. JONES

I had a client for a while, whom I'll refer to as Mrs. Jones. Now, she fancied herself a breeder of fine Persian cats. The trouble was, every kitten she brought in suffered from one of several maladies. In her kittens we usually found fleas, intestinal parasites, upper respiratory infections, the list could go on. Despite my best efforts at educating her on basic kitten husbandry and good nutrition, she continually brought in litters of kittens in less than perfect health or condition. Nonetheless, she always managed to find buyers for her kittens.

Now, I want to describe Mrs. Jones. She cared very little about her wardrobe, or for that matter, her personal hygiene. And she was a very loud person in her speaking. To quote one of my favorite movies, "She was so loud, you couldn't hear a dump truck driving through a nitroglycerin plant." We always treated her well and took good care of her cats... so fortunately or unfortunately, we kept her as a client.

On one occasion Mrs. Jones tried to show everyone in the office her scar from some recent surgery. Even other clients weren't immune to her attempts. While in the exam room she tried to lift her blouse and show me the scar. I had to talk fast and work even faster to get out of that situation. I learned fast that I'd always keep my technician in the room during her visits to try and avoid such embarrassing situations.

On another occasion, she was going on and on about her recent litter of kittens, which we were in the middle of being treated for fleas, coccidiosis, and an upper respiratory infection. She was once again very adamant and thought that they were the best she had ever produced. Mrs. Jones was talking in an even louder voice than usual and proclaimed to everyone within earshot, including those in the waiting room, "Dr. Migneco, we produce the most beautiful babies together."

Needless to say, I snuck out the back door of the exam room after that appointment.

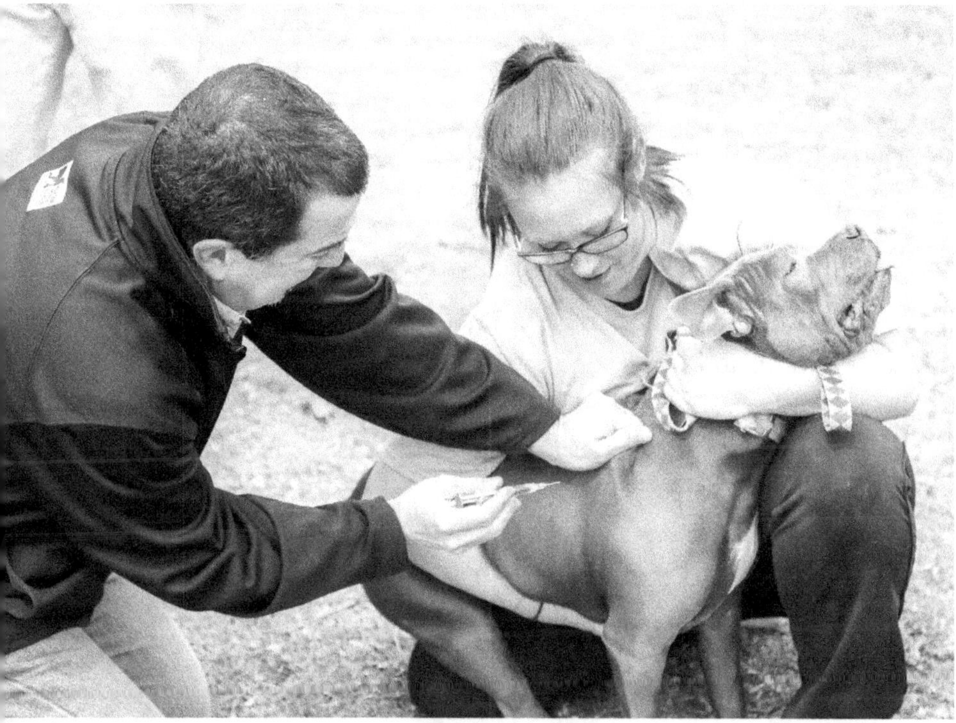

Vaccination clinic for the Animal Protective Association

LIGHTS OUT

Puppies chew. Sorry, but this is a fact of life. If you are considering getting a new puppy, be prepared for the inevitable chewing of some furniture, clothing, drapery, or other valuable household product. Clients consistently ask me how to get their puppy to stop chewing on things. I always say make sure the pup has plenty of toys that are appropriate for it to chew on, and then try diligently to avoid any opportunities for the pup to get into mischief. I know, easier said than done.

A young recently married couple, Jim and Brenda, who happened to be very good friends, purchased a very handsome German shepherd puppy as their first dog in their first house. They brought the puppy to me for vaccinations and to be neutered when the time came. It started to grow into a very good-looking specimen, representative of the proud bloodlines from which it was descended. But, just like babies who cry a lot while teething, puppies tend to chew a lot while teething.

My friends were starting to get frustrated with Dex, the new puppy. Meanwhile, he was perfectly content chewing on their new furniture, the woodwork in their new house, and anything else that happened to be close by whenever he got the urge to chew. At that time the couple worked out of the house, and Dex was becoming quite proficient at escaping out of the kitchen. A baby gate might have been strong enough to keep a human baby out, but not a baby German shepherd in. He even learned how to escape out of a crate which they had purchased for him.

I doled out the usual advice, but unfortunately the problem continued. At their wits end, Jim and Brenda finally settled on leaving Dex in the garage when he couldn't be supervised. This seemed to be a good solution as no new evidence of chewing could be found in the garage after a couple of trial periods. Of course, it could be that Dex was just starting to out of this obnoxious puppy phase.

Jim and Brenda and Dex's life settled down to a more normal routine. Dex seemed to grow up and he did indeed become that very handsome German shepherd dog we all thought he would. Then one night, Jim and Brenda had to go out together. They got into Jim's brand new car, pulled

out of the garage, and started to leave. Brenda asked Jim why he had not turned on the headlights. Jim assured her that he had, but both could not see any light coming from the front of the car. Since they were late for their engagement, they switched to Brenda's car and left Jim's car in the garage.

The next day, Jim examined the car in an attempt to figure out why the lights weren't working. Now, not every guy is mechanically inclined, but Jim knew his way around a car. He checked the usual suspects, such as a bad fuse, but couldn't find the cause. Finally he got on his back and crawled under the front end. What he found astounded him. Coming out of the back of both headlights were wires that had been gnawed on and pulled out of the attachments to the lights. It seemed Dex had somehow crawled under the car, reached up behind the front bumper, and chewed the wires coming out of both headlights.

It was quite a mystery why the dog had chosen to chew on these wires. Much less, how he had contorted his body to reach to reach them. Just when they thought the chewing problem was over, they now had a dog trying to eat their car. I can just imagine Jim going into work the next day and trying to explain why he needed new headlights. I'm sure he got a lot of trouble from his fellow workers. He did get a good deal on some new headlights though. I forgot to mention that Jim worked for Chrysler.

My co-worker at Gateway Pet Guardians, Sara Cordevant,
and I after rescuing kittens on community outreach (2019)

MY FAVRE(ITE) CLIENT

One of my favorite clients was Mrs. Favre, a regular client of ours since we first opened Hillside's clinic doors. Her original pet's name was Miss Kitty, and together, their visits could be both the highlight and lowlight of any day. She was one of those clients who complained about every penny she was charged. Not in a mean way, but just with subtle comments about how much we were charging her, or how I must be making a lot of money off of her. Of course, we took it all in stride and smiled more, trying to soften her up.

Mrs. Favre's husband usually drove her to the clinic for her pet visits. He was a thin wisp of a man who kept quiet in the corner and alternated between smiling at us and frowning at his wife. He did not have much to say, but knowing Mrs. Favre, this was not a surprise. He was French and I think an illustration of a stereotypical French man in a dictionary would be of him. He always wore a beret and had one of those very thin mustaches. His name was Rene, what else, but he reminded me of Marcel Marceau. Maybe it was that he did not have much to say as much as how he looked. He was a wonderful man though and I did enjoy his visits and talking to him when I could.

Their cat, Miss Kitty, was diagnosed with diabetes mellitus several years previously. She weighed about 19 pounds and had remained the same weight throughout her many visits. Despite my repeated admonitions to Mrs. Favre about her weight and her health, Miss Kitty never approached anywhere close to what I considered to be her ideal weight. According to Mrs. Favre, it was because she was a Maine Coot (I never could get her to understand that she meant Maine Coon, not Maine Coot), and is big-boned. Most veterinarians have heard this one before. ``My cat's not overweight, it's just a Maine Coon." I appreciated it even more because of Mrs. Favre's tilt on the name. Of course, her cat isn't a Maine Coon, but there is no arguing with her on that matter. To this day whenever I hear a client say their cat is a Maine Coon, I laugh about it.

Another matter that is of no use arguing about is Miss Kitty's age. Mrs. Favre was adamant that her cat was over 20 years old, although our

full medical records place her closer to 10. Alas, the evidence will never convince Mrs. Favre. To her credit, Mrs. Favre has kept her cat alive and well for the past five years, despite its medical condition and weight problem. I consider it a little bit of a trade-off. She manages to keep the cat alive, despite what I consider to be a failure on my part to get Miss Kitty to lose weight. But then again, I can't take all the blame; Mrs. Favre is the one who feeds the cat after all.

"Feeds the cat" is a phrase I use loosely. Miss Kitty is on a "See Food Diet," and she appears to have never seen a meal that she hasn't liked. Even better, Mrs. Favre provides her with ample chances to see plenty of meals. Miss Kitty has even managed to train Mrs. Favre to grab her a snack every morning at 2 am. The thing is, Mrs. Favre doesn't stop there. She continues to provide Miss Kitty her meals at 7 am, 2 pm, and 6 pm. She swears that the total amount fed throughout the day amounts to the prescribed amount of prescription diet we recommend, although her nice neighbor, who often later on brought her to the clinic for the visits, has a different story. Apparently, he's also witnessed Mrs. Favre's trips to the grocery store and her whopping purchases of 30-40 cans of cat food. I find it strange that she's never considered mentioning that.

Oh, and one more thing...why do some clients feel the need to tell us about the frequency and consistency of their pet's bowel movements? I am not talking about when there is diarrhea happening, I mean the pet's normal everyday bowel movements. Mrs. Favre seems to delight in giving the technicians and me great details of her cat's "movements" on every visit. We just chalk it up to her devotion to her cat and consider the source. No pun intended.

I actually did get a glimpse of Mrs. Favre's cat feeding habits when I originally met her. She had called the clinic to arrange a "house call" to vaccinate a couple of cats living in her basement. During the call, she advised me that they were a "little" wild. I did actually catch a glimpse or two of the cats as they scampered from one hiding place to the next, but that was as close as I got to them. It was like seeing "floaters," those random bits of movement in the corner of your eye without anything actually being there. I'd never seen cats move so fast. There would be no

vaccinations that day, that's for sure. But, something else caught my eye that day.

Mrs. Favre had set up a feeding station for the two cats in the basement where they lived. Two very large feeding bowls were filled to the brim with dry cat food. It was "free-choice" feeding to the max. It reminded me of the *Beverly Hillbillies'* episodes where Jethro Bodine ate his cornflakes by emptying the whole box into a mixing bowl. Those two bowls must have held a whole bag of cat food each.

Perhaps Miss Kitty was one of those cats I caught a glimpse of during our visit. Perhaps she ate to the point of being incapacitated, was too slow to avoid capture, and decided to resign herself to the inevitable? I guess we'll never know, considering Mrs. Favre still believes her cat is 20 years old. She also believes I'm James Herriot. Why spoil her fantasy? I just wish she treated me the way Tricki Woo treated his Uncle Herriot.

Now here is the rest of the story: after her husband died, Mrs. Favre was always brought to the clinic by her neighbor. He was a lawyer and whenever she started to complain about her bill, he would be standing behind her shaking his head and smiling. Apparently, he knew something I didn't. Several years after her death, I read that The Katherine Favre Foundation for Animals, donated $5 million dollars to the local humane society. This was the same humane society located one block north of my clinic. The same clinic that she visited and the clinic that took care of her cats for many years. The clinic where she complained on every visit about every dollar she spent. Now I know why she complained about the money every time she came in. She was socking it away for a rainy day. Seriously though, I am not upset at all about what she did with her money. It was her money to do with whatever she wanted. It went to a good cause and her foundation continues to help the animal welfare community to this day. Oh, and the head of the foundation is the lawyer who used to drive her to the clinic. He does a great job continuing to spread the wealth of her generosity.

I just wish that she had read *All Creatures Great and Small* and the story of Tricki Woo before she passed.

My daughter Nina and I in the Boundary Waters Canoe Area,
Minnesota during our father-daughter canoe trip (2016)

DEATH IS FINAL.
OR IS IT?

Dealing with death is common when you work at a veterinary clinic. Not that we have animals dying every day, but we do deal with the passing of animals, whether it be from old age, sickness, trauma, or natural causes. It never gets easy dealing with death, but we seem to handle it a lot better than some of our clients do.

Veterinarians have the profound responsibility of guiding owners when the time has come to say goodbye to their pets. We never want to make that decision for the owners, but we can educate them on their pet's quality of life and when it may be the appropriate time to end suffering. Owners, however, commonly want me to make the decision for them by asking, "What would you do?" I always try to ease the burden by reminding them that this difficult decision is being made on the pet's behalf. I like to tell them, "It is okay to be sad, just don't feel bad about the brave decision you're making."

But some people cannot bring themselves to make that hard decision. I've had clients keep their pets alive for their own sake, and not for that of the pet. It is really difficult to see animals in obvious pain and suffering, and not be allowed to bring them to a peaceful end. I do everything I can to get the client to see that it is in the pet's best interest.

Even after a pet has died, sometimes clients have a difficult time accepting it. Once a family with multiple pets had a very elderly dog whose time had come. They were very good pet owners and requested home euthanasia, a service we provide where the pet is put to sleep in its own home. This avoids the stress that a lot of animals feel when going to the clinic, so that their final day is as stress-free as possible.

My technician and I went to their home and performed the euthanasia. After allowing the family to say their goodbyes, it was time to leave. We always discuss ahead of time about the disposition of the remains after the euthanasia. The owners had indicated that they were interested in cremation and having the ashes returned to them. A lot of clients

request this so they can bury the ashes in the yard or keep them in a nice urn. But when it was time to leave, the owners informed us that they wanted to keep the dog's body for several days to allow for closure for themselves and the other pets in the house.

I was a little confused, but the clients explained that they were planning to keep the dog's body in the family room, on a blanket for a few days so that the other dogs and cats could have time for goodbyes. It also allowed them more time for closure. Of course, I did not think this was a good idea for several reasons, the most important of which being that it was the middle of summer, but I kept my mouth shut and said goodbye.

Three days later the owners brought the dog's body into the clinic for cremation. I could only imagine what their house must have smelled like after getting close to the dog. I mean, it wasn't like they lived in an igloo. I am glad they got their closure, but the only closure I was interested in at that point was the twist tie on the bag the dog was in.

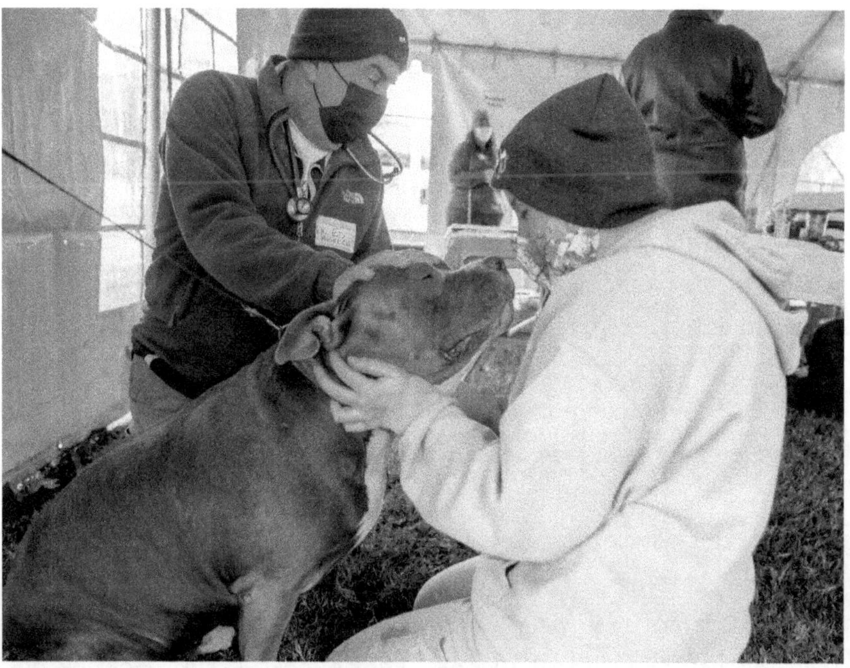

Vaccination clinic during Covid-19 times (2021),
with CVT Kat Dowling

YOU CAN'T MAKE THIS UP

My mom used to say 'You can't make this up," when referring to the crazy things we used to see and hear at the clinic. Here are some questions relayed by clients. Try not to shake your head while reading them.

1. "I am in Colorado and my dog is squinting. Could his eyes be dry?"
"I don't know, could the sun be in his eyes?"

2. "The medicine you gave my cat made his eyes get big. Is that normal?"
"Yes, it is okay, so don't worry." "That's good, but the cat escaped outside and I can't find him. Should I continue to give the medicine? Is it bad if he doesn't get the medicine?" "Does it matter since the cat is not to be found anyway?"

3. An owner called to ask why her neutered male cat was "humping" both her hand and arm and what she could do to prevent that from ever happening again. I recommended washing her hands before she came into the clinic. The owner changed her mind and said, "I'm actually going to the local Halloween costume store to buy the cat a fake hand to have fun with."

4. An owner called to say her 18-year-old cat, which was near death before starting medication I had prescribed, was doing great. The cat was eating and drinking and playing again. She wanted to know if her cat should stay on the medicine. I told the owner it was okay to stop the medicine if they thought 18 years was enough. If they wanted to try for 19 or 20, then they should continue the medication as directed.

5. Someone called to say that their dog had died, and in the meantime, they'd been keeping him in the freezer. Every night they took the dog out of the freezer and let it "sleep" in bed with them. They wanted to know how long they could keep doing this. "I don't know," I said. "How low do you keep the AC on at night?"

6. A client called frantically to the clinic saying, "I think my dog is dying. He's paralyzed, can't get up, and is breathing very fast."
"Can you bring him in right away?" "No, I am at work right now.

7. "That E-collar you put in my dog is driving him crazy. He cannot settle down, is very restless, and is bothered by it all the time. He's also keeping us up at night." "Do you want to bring the dog in for us to check him out and look for alternative solutions?" "Well, not right now, he's sleeping."

8. "I can't keep my dog off of my bed at night. He always ends up sleeping on my legs. Besides keeping me awake he is leaving bruises all over my legs." "What type of dog do you have?" "A Chihuahua."

9. "I want to bring my dog in today, she's having diarrhea." "Can you bring in a stool sample when you come in?" "No, I can't tell which one is from which dog in the yard."

10. After spending thousands of dollars on an expensive orthopedic surgery, a client brought the dog in only for us to discover the metal implant had broken down and the surgery would have to be repeated. We questioned her, "Why did you let your dog go out and chase squirrels after the very expensive orthopedic surgery he had?" " I thought it was okay since he would hold the leg up anyway while chasing the squirrels."

11. A client said that their dog was too old to have the surgery that was recommended. I agreed and said, "Yes, we should wait till he's younger."

12. A client stated that their dog did not like to have alcohol/vinegar solution poured into its very inflamed ear. Sometimes you just have to say, "No shit."

IT'S NOT WHAT YOU THINK

Once I was asked by a friend if I'd do a consultation on the pet of her assistant, Michelle. My friend's assistant scheduled an appointment with me because she'd found a small lump on the dog and was told by her previous vet that it was cancer. Any time a client receives a diagnosis of possible cancer in their pet, it can be upsetting. I am always willing to offer a second opinion in a professional manner, and of course I was happy to be of assistance to my friend at the same time.

I examined the dog and found the before-mentioned lump. Then I performed a fine needle aspirate procedure where I extracted a few cells from the lump to examine under the microscope. This is an attempt to determine the lump's identity and the best method to treat it. I was able to determine that the lump was a mast cell tumor, which is very common in dogs and easily diagnosed.

I explained the best options for treating mast cell tumors, recommending surgical removal of the lump. With this type of tumor, it is necessary to make very wide surgical margins into what appears to be normal tissue, because tumor cells can extend out beyond the obvious lump, into the normal-looking tissue. Our team would send off the tissue sample to a pathologist for a definitive diagnosis and to determine if the margins were 'clean.' Meaning, he would look to see if I had removed all of the tumor. If there were tumor cells out to the margin, it could mean additional surgery.

I carefully explained to Michelle that this type of tumor is commonly cured by surgical excision alone, but it can be hard for a client to understand why there's such a long incision to remove a small lump. I actually like to say to clients that the length of an incision does not matter, because healing occurs side to side, not lengthwise. Explaining the nuts and bolts ahead of time is very crucial to the owner's understanding of their dog's medical needs, and their satisfaction with the job you do.

The surgery went without a hitch and the dog recovered wonderfully. Several days later, I received a great report from the pathologist that the tumor was completely removed, and we had clean margins. I relayed

all of this to Michelle, and of course, she was very happy. And I scored some points with my friend

Now it happens that we were all at the same social gathering the following week. At a very loud bar with several hundred people drinking and having a good time, I ran into my new client Michelle, who introduced me to her boyfriend as the doctor who "saved their dog's life." He tried to thank me, but it was too loud in the bar area to have a real conversation. I said you're welcome, shaking my head several times, not really hearing anything he said.

Later in the evening, I retreated into the much quieter men's room. As I was standing at the urinal, Michelle's boyfriend walked into the restroom and stood two urinals away from me. Once again, he proceeded to thank me for helping out their dog. It was right at this moment that another gentleman came in and stood at the urinal between us. Unfortunately, the third gentleman came in at the same exact time the boyfriend said, "I am sure glad that thing came out clean."

Obviously, I knew he was talking about the tumor and its margins. Just as obviously, the third gentleman didn't comprehend and said, "Excuse me, I think I will just leave you two alone now," and walked out of the restroom rather quickly. I wanted to say, "It's not what you think," but I wasn't fast enough. At that point, I wish it had been as loud in the restroom as it was in the bustling bar.

I did not enjoy myself the rest of the evening, as I kept looking around to see if anyone was looking my way, pointing or laughing or staring. I kept saying over and over in my mind, "It's really not what you think!!"

SAY IT LIKE YOU MEAN IT

I like to think that I have a good rapport with clients in the exam room. I learned a great deal about the importance of a doctor-client relationship during the early years observing Dr. Schmelzer. His clients loved him and he always had a joke ready, especially for the kids accompanying their parents. To this day, I find myself repeating the same jokes he told over 40 years ago.

After I'm done vaccinating a family pet, I like to casually ask any children in the room what arm they'd prefer for their vaccination. It's not unusual for them to start rolling up their sleeve before they catch themselves and pull back in horror. I always reassure them that I was just kidding with them and meant no harm.

My humor isn't only reserved for the kids. Occasionally when I'm examining the ears of a patient, I ask the owner to look into the opposite ear and let me know when they see the light from the otoscope as I examine the other side. Several times I have to pause for effect, as the owners don't always catch my drift and continue intently searching for a light in the opposite ear. After I'm fully entertained, I slyly drop a joke that there must be something blocking the light traveling from one side to the other.

In my new role as a shelter vet for Gateway Pet Guardians, we host drive-through vaccination clinics in an attempt to get more animals vaccinated and increase herd immunity in our community. I realize not everyone is not enamored with that style of veterinary medicine, but I have come to realize it's importance while working in the trenches. Not everyone can afford the best care for their pets, but that does not mean they do not love them. Anyway, I always try to have fun when doing these events.

At least once every clinic, I walk up to someone with a very cute little dog in their arms and I say that there must be some sort of mistake, since we are only vaccinating cute dogs today. Of course, they know right away I am kidding and am actually complimenting their dog. It always brings a laugh and a smile to their face.

At these clinics we usually see the typical pit bull or mixes common in our area, or it goes to the opposite extreme and the owners have tiny little terriers or Shih Tzus. In this case invariably it is some large man who is carrying the dog lovingly in his arms while the wife drives the car. I always wonder why the largest, toughest guys have the tiniest dogs. After vaccinating the dog being held by the husband, I will turn to the wife and ask her if she would like the "other big dog" vaccinated today.

My other go-to joke while directing the cars pulling into the parking lot for the drive-thru clinic is to bang on the hood of the car slightly, and let the driver think that they have pulled too far forward and run into me. Their eyes will get really big, and then I walk around the car and let them in on the joke. If I am going to be out in 90-degree weather for a couple of hours, I might as well enjoy myself.

I may not portray the image of the staid professional doctor to some people. But I am a believer that if your clients are at ease, then they are more likely to respond to you. If they like you and you make them comfortable, they are more likely to listen to your recommendations. I do have a good reputation for keeping clients once they meet me and developing a deep bond with them. I guess you could say it's a case of "Laughter is the best medicine."

WHAT WAS I GOING TO SAY?

I am taking part in a lifetime study of the children whose parents have Alzheimer's Disease. True story in that I missed my last appointment. I forgot about it. Wonder if I should be worried.

MUSINGS

WHEN THEY SAY THIS... THEY MEAN THAT

Trivia is one of my favorite pastimes, as trivia nights are common events around St. Louis, used as a method of raising money for a charitable organization. There's something exhilarating about somehow knowing the answer to an obscure question, surprising both you and your friends who paid witness to this random act of "genius." My friend Mark and I like to shoot movie quotes back and forth at each other, testing our cinematic knowledge, whenever we are together. One of my specialties is being "The Predictor," offering up answers to questions that haven't been asked yet. At trivia nights, I've been known to come up with the answers to possible questions after only hearing the category for the next round. Sometimes this trick even carries over to work.

After some 30 years of practice, I've reached the point where I can view the appointment book and make a diagnosis before seeing the animal. Of course I am kidding, but certain entries made in the notes section of an appointment hint at what is most likely going on with the animal. My staff elicits these statements from clients who call in. It is important to know ahead of time why an animal is being brought into the clinic, as it helps us prepare what we may need for the appointment.

For example, when I see that a cat is coming in for a "broken leg," this is most likely going to be a cat bite abscess, which can be extremely painful and will cause the cat to stop using the affected limb. One of the first things we do during the course of an examination is to take the cat's body temperature. If the temperature is elevated, I usually start the search for the elusive bite marks hidden under the fur. It's especially rewarding to finally spot the paired bite marks, as a bite wound almost always is caused by two teeth. Not that I particularly enjoy abscesses, but they are a heck of a lot easier to deal with than a broken leg.

We commonly get phone calls from clients, particularly people who've never been into our clinic before, saying that their puppy is sick, and they're sure that it was "poisoned." It seems their new puppy, which they spent a large sum of money to purchase, but that has not been seen by a veterinarian since being purchased, is now vomiting and has bloody

diarrhea. It just has to have been poisoned by some malicious neighbor or animal hater. Anyone with any veterinary medicine experience
realizes that I am talking about canine parvovirus, a particularly serious
viral disease of dogs that causes vomiting and bloody diarrhea as previously described. It seemingly occurs suddenly, although it has been
incubating in the body for several days. The sad part is that parvovirus
is preventable if the new puppy is vaccinated--even sadder part is that
we aren't always able to save the pup, as there are no drugs that directly
kill the virus. Despite intensive supportive care including fluid therapy
and medicine for the vomiting, the pup only recovers if they are strong
enough for their body to get rid of the virus. While poisonings do occur
rarely, more commonly we see needless disease and death due to an
owner's lack of education about proper vaccinations.

Another phone call which triggers an almost immediate diagnosis is one in which the owner says their dog has had a "stroke." A typical scenario is owners who wake up and find their geriatric dog unable to walk, maybe stumbling to one side, with a head tilt. Both the dog and the owners can be very distressed. Whenever I hear about an appointment involving a possible stroke, this is going to be a dog suffering from Idiopathic Geriatric Vestibular Syndrome until proven otherwise. This syndrome involves the vestibular nerve, in the inner ear, which is involved in maintaining balance. The nerve becomes inflamed suddenly, and the dog can suffer from vertigo, imbalance, and even nausea and vomiting. "Idiopathic" is a fancy word for unknown, meaning that when they looked at a large number of cases of this condition, and ruled out obvious known causes like ear infections, the majority of cases were attributed to an unknown cause. The good news is that this is generally a self-limiting condition, and the dog can make a complete recovery, usually within a day or two.

We also commonly get appointments for dogs who supposedly have "broken legs." This can be a stumper, because I have to ask a couple of questions of the owner before I examine the dog for a diagnosis. As soon as I hear the owner say that the dog was running in the backyard and came up acutely lame, I can say with reasonable certainty that the dog has suffered an ACL (anterior cruciate ligament) tear. This is unfortunately a very common canine orthopedic problem, and we deal with it almost on a weekly basis. It requires a surgical repair to stabilize the knee joint and to prevent arthritis from becoming an issue down the road. We always confirm the diagnosis with sedation and radiographs before discussing the surgical care with the owners. Veterinary radiologists tell us that they can diagnose an ACL tear just by looking at the radiographs. But we like to think that this is one time that general practitioners may actually be smarter than radiology specialists. While both of us may be able to come up with the most-likely diagnosis, we can usually do so over the phone.

My good friend, Dr. Matt Sturmer and I, on a trip to San Juan islands (2018)

CLIENT STORIES

AIN'T NO SUNSHINE

A mondegreen is a misunderstood or misinterpreted word or phrase resulting from a mishearing of the lyrics of a song. An example would be, "There's a bathroom on the right," instead of "There's a bad moon on the rise," from Creedence Clearwater Revival. Or "The girl with colitis goes by," instead of 'The girl with kaleidoscope eyes," from the Beatles. I actually prepared the questions for a trivia night one time where I made up one category with 10 different mondegreens, and the participants had to guess the correct lyrics and the song they came from. If you bear with me, you will see why this title came to mind at this time.

I mentioned how these stories will undoubtedly be familiar to other veterinarians. In fact, I'm convinced that every day across the country, clinics handle the same scenarios, just with the names changed to protect the innocent. This story, in one form or another, has assuredly been replayed elsewhere. It's not until it happens to you, that you actually believe it's true.

My associate was examining a young puppy that belonged to a new client. The puppy was brought in because it incessantly dragged its rear across the floor. Now, every veterinarian in the world knows that the most common cause of this condition would be anal sac impaction. Or as James Herriot would say, "Flop-Bott," in the case of Tricki Woo. My associate, thorough veterinarian that she is, examined the puppy, and then proceeded to engage the client with some questions.

"There are several possible causes for a puppy to drag its rear end like this," my associate explained.

"Intestinal parasitism, which is common in puppies, or a food allergy

can make their rear end itch...or most commonly an anal sac problem."

"Well," exclaimed the owner with a very surprised look on her face, "I know it can't be the last thing you mentioned because my puppy is only three months old, and is still a virgin! She's much too young to be having such a problem."

My associate wasn't quite sure, but she assumed the client didn't hear her correctly. At that point, you make the decision whether or not to point out the client's mistake, which runs the risk of embarrassing her. So, Dr. Sherry started talking about the anal sacs, how they are located at the four and eight o'clock position around the anus, and how they can become impacted, making the animal uncomfortable. With each new piece of information, the client's face gradually became redder as she slowly realized her mistake.

The client finally admitted that she thought Dr. Sherry said, "anal sex" was the cause of her dog's problems. Not having ever owned a dog before, she thought that diagnosis seemed a little strange, but who was she to argue? The owner was just glad it was not a serious issue and that the puppy would be fine.

Which brings me back to the beginning of this story. There is a great song by Bill Withers. Boy, could he ever hold a note. Anyway, the song in question in called "Ain't No Sunshine." A good friend of mine admitted that for the longest time he thought the title was "Anal Sunshine." He always thought that was a rather risqué title for a pop song, so he was embarrassed to sing along. He was very relieved when I pointed out the mondegreen he had been experiencing. The good news is the puppy, and my friend, are just fine now. I guess you could say "It all worked out in the end." Or in this case, the puppy's end.

DON'T LEAVE ME HANGING

Today I had an appointment with a long-time client whom I had not seen since we had to put his 15-year-old dog to sleep last year. We got his dog through some serious health issues and he was extremely grateful for the time they had together. It had been several months since the tearful day when we all said goodbye to his beloved dog, so I was pleasantly surprised when I saw his name on the schedule for a puppy appointment. As I walked into the exam room, he said the exact thing that I was thinking. He asked if I was ready for another 15 years of visits from him. While I was excited to see his new pup, I told him that I could not say for sure that I would be around for the next 15 years in practice, but that the clinic would so he could expect the same high level of personal and professional care he experienced in the past.

While playing with and examining the new pup, he reminded me of the first time we met with his other dog, during an emergency, or at least a perceived emergency. He was at home hanging a picture, when he accidentally dropped one of those little picture-hanging hooks on the ground. His dog was nearby and immediately gobbled it up and swallowed it. He thought for sure he had caused his dog irreparable harm and was extremely upset as he told us the story. The physical exam was pretty unremarkable, and the dog looked happy and healthy. But because of the history from the client, I suggested an abdominal radiograph to find out if the hook had indeed been swallowed and would cause any problems.

We took a couple of radiographs to ascertain if the hook was present and where it was in the abdomen. It was indeed there but it was a very small hook and, in our estimation, would probably pass through the intestines without any trouble, as it did not have any sharp points, and the dog was rather large size. I took the radiograph into the exam room and showed the client to calm his fears and give him piece of mind.

I guess I made a good impression with that appointment as it led to 15 years of caring for that same dog. Today my client reminded me of what I said that first day when we met over the swallowed picture hook. Appar-

ently, I showed the client the radiograph, with the metallic hook clearly visible in the abdomen, and said, "Your dog is the picture of health." I honestly had not remembered until the client reminded me but it does sound like something I would say. I guess it worked for the client as it was the start of a long relationship. And as for the hook, it did indeed pass with no problems. I guess that I hooked a client for life that day.

MOONSTRUCK

In the spring of the year, it is kitten season and it is all hands on deck. One particular day we had a total of 38 kittens in our cat room, and all were in need of veterinary care. The cat team carefully tries to select unique names for all of the kittens, and especially if there is a litter, to give them all corresponding names. Like the months of the year, or famous siblings, etc. Trying to keep them all straight, and not duplicate any veterinary care, etc., can be a daunting task. One solo kitten that was suffering from diarrhea was given the name Emore. I am not sure what the significance of the name is but is pronounced just like it looks. I looked at Sara, pointed to the kitten's cage, and said, "That's Emore". She looked at me with a pained look on her face, pointing to the cage in question and said, yes, "This one is Emore", because we had just got done working on that kitten. Notice please that I was not asking a question but making a statement. In my best Dean Martin voice I broke out in song. "When the poop starts to fly and it looks like mud pie, that's Emore".

WAKE ME, I MUST BE DREAMING

The type of care owners provide for their pet varies greatly. Some "pets" don't receive any regular veterinary care. A large number of owners bring in their pets only for required services and nothing else. A few owners go the extra mile when it comes to their pets, bringing them in whenever they feel like something is wrong. And finally, there are pet owners such as the one I'm going to tell you about.

Benny was a neutered male Pug owned by one of our best clients. The client was a single young woman, and Benny was the most important thing in her life. He was brought in regularly for checkups, or when his owner believed something was seriously amiss, such as missing one meal, or having coughed once, or God forbid, sneezed. So, it was a very big deal when Benny woke up one day and had difficulty walking.

My team examined Benny that day and found him to be in pain whenever he tried to move his neck. He was also stumbling a bit and dragging one of his rear legs as he walked. The short version of the story is that we diagnosed Benny with Intervertebral Disc Disease. This means he had a bulging disc between two of the vertebrae in his neck. The bulging disc was causing pain and a small amount of neurologic dysfunction with his rear legs. We thought his prognosis for recovery was fine with medications, rest, time, and without the need for surgery.

I very carefully explained Benny's condition to his owner, along with a treatment plan and expected outcome and prognosis. She's one of those owners whom despite how long I took in the exam room to explain things, I knew to expect a phone call or two later. No sooner had Benny gone home, I received a phone call with some more questions. I once again went over all of the instructions I had given earlier and reassured the owner that I expected a full recovery.

Benny did progress and was well on his way to making a full recovery. This all occurred over several weeks, during which there were multiple phone calls and rechecks for the slightest hiccup. But one day, the scales tipped to an extreme level.

I had been unavailable when the owner tried to reach me during the

previous evening (thank you very much), and she had taken Benny to the emergency clinic in the middle of the night. We always receive a form from the emergency clinic the next day informing us of what occurred and what treatments, if any, the patient had undergone. On the form under "Presenting Complaint," the owner had written, "The dog was breathing rapidly and paddling his legs…" Now, this sentence would make a lot of us think the owner was perfectly justified in rushing the dog to the ER. But it was the last part of the sentence that made me happy I was unreachable.

The complete sentence read: "The dog was breathing rapidly and paddling his legs while sleeping soundly." I can just imagine the scene. Here was Benny, sleeping deeply, and probably chasing some squirrel in his dreams, when he's violently shaken awake to be taken to the ER. "Wake up Benny, we have to go to the emergency clinic!" I can't help but think of The Three Stooges when Curly is sound asleep and snoring very loudly, and Moe slaps him and says, "Wake up and go to sleep."

My daughter Nina and I on community outreach for Gateway Pet Guardians

WILL THE REAL RACHEL PRICE PLEASE STAND UP?

It happens often that a client will show up at the front desk wanting to know if I had a minute for a question. My front office staff is usually good at weeding out the serious inquiries from those that could be handled by other staff members. If I were to have to answer every single question or problem that arose during the course of a day, I would not have the time to actually practice medicine. We strive to make sure our clients know that we also take their pet's problems seriously, even if sometimes we have to say, "The doctor cannot come to the phone to talk to you right now." One of my vet school classmates bought a boat and named it "Consultation," so his staff could say the doctor was out on Consultation.

One day my receptionist told me that a client named Rachel Price was up front with a question. I knew that Rachel had dropped off her dog for surgery and assumed she was picking her up. It was my scheduled surgery day, and we always call the owners after their pets are out of anesthesia so they don't worry. But if I am available, I still like to see the owners at time of discharge to see if they have any questions.

As I rounded the corner towards the front lobby, I could see several people, including Rachel, standing at the counter. Next to Rachel was another young lady about the same age and height, who I also recognized. It took me a quick second to realize what was happening here, that standing next to Rachel Price, was another client named Rachel Price, who was here to pick up some medicine.

It's not that uncommon to have clients with the same name, but how often do they end up standing right next to each other without realizing it? I had sized up the situation quickly and decided to have a little fun. I walked to the front desk, where the two ladies were standing, stood behind them, and asked to speak to Rachel Price. Of course, they both turned around at the same time and responded, "Hello, I'm Rachel Price." I just smiled as they then turned towards each other with quizzical looks

on their faces. It was then that I said, "Rachel Price, meet Rachel Price."

After the introductions and some pleasantries, I got down to business and discharged Rachel's dog to her. But then I started to think about what it would have been like to have both Rachel Prices drop off their dogs for surgery on the same day. I wonder if their dogs have the same name? Or look alike? What if they were here to have the same procedure done? It could have been a logistical nightmare. We would have to make sure that we had "The Price is Right."

My daughters Anna and Gina with my mother, Virginia

OVER VERA-FICATION

Vera Bradley. Those two words have been known to make women weak in the knees and lighter in the pocketbook, even if that pocketbook looks great. As far as men go, those two words don't carry the same significance. Most men probably could not tell you if Vera Bradley was the latest winner of *American Idol*, the latest Bachelorette, or the designer of fashionable bags of all kinds. Unless of course he happens to be a father of three girls. Then he knows. Believe me, he knows. One of my daughters once had the nerve to ask for a Vera Bradley laundry bag. Really? A designer bag to carry her dirty laundry home from college so her mother or I could do it for her? She got quite the dirty look from me because of that request.

One day one of our favorite clients came into the clinic with a very nice, familiar-looking bag slung over her shoulder. All work at the front desk came to a halt as my staff gathered to admire the bag. I could just imagine that the compliments were flowing even before they managed to ask the client why she had come in that day. But then her cat poked its head out of the top of the bag. It seems the cat had commandeered the bag as her own when the client brought it home one day. The cat preferred the bag over its carrier and would allow the owner to take it anywhere in the bag, including the veterinary office. It really makes our job easier when a cat comes in happy.

The cat was actually coming in for some blood work so the client allowed us to take the cat to the treatment room, where I set the bag on the table, reached in and extracted the serene patient. As I set the cat on the table, I immediately took a step back, hit myself in the forehead with the palm of my hand, and exclaimed, "I can't believe that I just did that!" My staff looked at me unsure of what I was talking about. So, I repeated, "I can't believe I did that!" "I let the cat out of the bag." My staff is used to my stupid jokes and just groaned, while I was actually proud of my quick wit.

We shaved its neck and obtained the necessary blood sample with ease from the peaceful cat. The client waited in the exam room, with the

cat sleeping peacefully in the Vera Bradley bag while the tests were run. We were able to go back into the room after only a short while to tell her the good news that the test results were all normal. We accompanied her to the front desk to check out, where of course there were more comments and jealousy about "The Bag."

At our next staff meeting we were discussing our attempts to make our practice a "Cat Friendly Practice." This national campaign is attempting to increase the number of cat visits to veterinary clinics by making each practice visit an easier affair for the client and the cat. While we are always trying to come up with new ways to increase compliance among our cat clients, I had to draw the line with the suggestion of buying our clients Vera Bradley bags to bring their cats in. I did not think we could justify the expense, but the idea to design and market Vera Bradley cat carriers is being mulled over.

Meeting new friends on my trip to Machu Picchu

I GET A CHARGE OUT OF YOU

If you practice long enough, every once in a while, a case will walk through your door that will surprise you. Actually, in veterinary medicine it probably happens more than we realize. That was the situation with Millie, a rescue dog that was being fostered by one of our clients, Jill. Jill was fostering Millie for Gateway Pet Guardians. It just so happened that many years later Jill ended up helping me with the layout for this book, and she reminded me of the case during one of our meetings. I had not thought about Millie for a long time. But the memories came flooding back to me.

One day Jill heard a commotion in the bedroom while she was asleep. She heard a thumping noise and Millie thrashing on the floor like she was having a seizure. She ran to her side and found Millie, breathing rapidly and obviously in some distress. Next to Millie there was the cord from the TV, blackened and charred in the middle. Putting two and two together, Jill surmised correctly that Millie must have bitten the cord and been electrocuted. She scooped Millie up into her arms and rushed her over to our clinic.

The scenario described by Jill, and resulting clinical signs we found when Millie was examined, were typical for cats and dogs who bite an electrical cord. Across the roof of Millie's mouth, on the hard palate, was a linear burn stretching from one side to the other. We quickly assessed her condition, and started treatment for shock and pain. A common side effect of this type of electric shock is the development of pulmonary edema, or fluid accumulation in the lungs secondary to the inflammation and shock. Millie followed the textbooks in this regard and did indeed develop pulmonary edema and difficulty breathing.

Millie ended up spending a couple of days in our hospital, on medication to relieve her pain and also to help resolve the pulmonary edema. It was a tense time for Jill and for us also. I am happy to say that Millie went on to make a full recovery, and even ended up being adopted by Jill. So, we were able to continue to see her for many more years.

The clinical presentation and clinical signs that Millie presented for after suffering an electrical shock were exactly like the syndrome is described in those thick textbooks that I like to collect. But the point is, that up until that point in time, this was a condition that I had only read about. Up until that moment, I had not ever seen a case of electric shock, much less treated one. But when the time came, the staff and I knew what to do and reacted promptly and accurately. I guess you could say we will be ready in case lightning strikes twice.

Millie

EMPLOYEE STORIES

WHEN I DRINK ALONE, I PREFER TO BE BY MYSELF

A new client came into our clinic with three brand new, very cute Akita puppies. He was very proud of them, as they were going to be guard dogs for his new business, a car repair garage. Perhaps you could tell from some of my other stories that I am not the biggest fans of Akitas. But these dogs were the exception to my rule. Maybe getting to know these dogs from an early age I was able to come to some sort of understanding with them. Or maybe because of what happened in this story, they considered me their buddy, or drinking buddy.

Over the next few months, we saw the client and his puppies several more times and watched them grow into handsome dogs. One day when the pups were about five months old, the client frantically called the clinic. Someone had left a bucket of antifreeze unattended in the garage overnight and the pups had helped themselves to the tasty liquid. Despite being toxic to dogs and humans, antifreeze has a pleasant taste. You would think the manufacturers could solve this by adding something to it to make it taste bad. It was difficult to say exactly how much was ingested, or even if all three dogs had done so, but he believed that the bucket originally contained a large amount of antifreeze. We advised him to bring the dogs over right away and we immediately started to prepare what we'd need to treat their toxicosis.

When he arrived, we carefully explained exactly how we'd treat the dogs. It may seem strange, but during that time the only treatment to combat poisoning by antifreeze was to give the dogs pure grain alcohol intravenously. Antifreeze becomes toxic only after the body starts to metabolize it and break it down. It is the byproducts of the antifreeze metabolism that are actually deadly. By giving pure grain alcohol to the dogs, their bodies will preferentially metabolize the alcohol first, and the antifreeze would be eliminated from their bodies unchanged, thus

causing no harm. The alcohol and antifreeze are both metabolized by the same pathway in the body, and by keeping it occupied with the alcohol, the antifreeze is excreted unchanged, and therefore, rendered non-toxic.

We explained to the owner that the prognosis for these pups was guarded at best, but that our team would do everything possible to save his dogs. We immediately established intravenous catheters and began fluid therapy on each dog. None of the dogs had yet shown any clinical signs of toxicity. Then we carefully calculated the dose of alcohol for each dog and delivered the individual doses intravenously.

It's a strange sight to witness the dogs' reactions to this specific treatment. It's basically inducing immediate, complete drunkenness within a few minutes after giving the injection of alcohol. They start to wobble, get unsteady, and fall into a deep, alcohol-induced sleep. Before long, the clinic was filled with the sound of snoring Akitas.

The treatment is repeated every four to six hours at first, and then slowly tapered off over the course of a few days. The good news is that all three pups recovered and were eventually sent home. I'm sure it was some hangover they all had after two full days of intravenous alcohol therapy. Talk about a bender.

When I first received the call from the client, I realized that we did not have any pure grain alcohol in the clinic. It's just not something you tend to keep around. So, I sent my mother, who was also my receptionist, down to the 24-hour liquor store on the corner to purchase some. As social and gregarious as my mother is, she enjoyed trying to explain to the clerk that the two, two-liter bottles of pure grain alcohol she happened to be buying at eight o'clock in the morning was for medicinal purposes. He just smiled and said "Sure lady, whatever you say." She said, "No, you really don't understand," and again tried to tell him all about the sick puppies and what the liquor was really being used for. The clerk just politely smiled and said, "And if the dogs need their daily dose of vitamin C, you'll find the orange juice in the cooler over there."

PORK ON THE HOOF

The area where I live and practice is called the Hill. It is actually the highest point in the city of St. Louis. It is also the area where Italian immigrants settled in the late 1800's and early 1900's as they immigrated to America. To this day the neighborhood has maintained its Italian heritage, with a rich variety of delis, restaurants, and bakeries. It is a wonderful place to live and raise a family.

Living in the same neighborhood where I practice has certain advantages. I love to take walks, and it is not unusual to see many of my patients and clients as I walk around. Sometimes I joke that I can actually perform "rounds" and check up on my patients while on my walks around the neighborhood. It also gives you a good feeling to hear people call out to you. "Hello Dr. Ed, how are all the sick animals doing?" is a common greeting I would hear. It took a few years, but I really feel like I am accepted in this tight-knit community.

At the same time, living and working in such close proximity does have a few drawbacks. Since my neighbors know where I live, and what I do for a living, I have become the unofficial animal control officer of the Hill. Every stray dog or cat that is found seems to end up on my doorstep. My neighbors seem to think that I should be able to instantly recognize every stray animal, and pull up from memory its name, address, and phone number.

My duties as unofficial animal control officer was really put to the test when I received a phone call one night from my office manager, Jan, who also happens to live in the neighborhood. She informed me that there were two pigs in her alley. I replied, "That's nice," knowing full well what she really wanted from me. But, sometimes you just have to make the person vocalize the request. She asked if I could come over and retrieve the pigs before they got hurt. "Why not?" I replied. All I would miss was reruns of *ADAM-12* on TV.

When I reached Jan's house, she led me out to her alley where I saw two police cars and two uniformed officers running around. I remembered her comments about there being two pigs in the alley, and ques-

tioned her choice of words, considering that we usually had a good relationship with the police in our district. But then she pointed out the two baby Pot-Bellied Pigs that the two officers were trying to corral. I actually hung back for a minute or two and enjoyed watching the officers. It reminded me of the movie *Rocky II* when he tries to catch the chicken during his training. The baby pigs proved to be too much of a match for the frustrated officers. You would have thought the pigs were covered with grease and this was a county fair as many times as they slipped out of the officers hands.

Pretty soon, another car pulled up containing a police captain who happened to be in the area and had heard the call on the radio. Riding along with him for some reason was a priest. Anyway, the captain was not about to get out of his car and be embarrassed by the escapist pigs. I would have loved to have heard what he and the priest were saying at this time. There is a joke there somewhere. A police captain and a priest drive up in an alley…

Finally, I very carefully asked the officers if I could give it a try. They both were breathing rather fast and just said good luck. In vet school, you do get some experience working with pigs. Even though I knew back then that I would not be doing this for a living, the knowledge had not totally escaped me. And my former father-in-law was a pig farmer for a while and during visits I did get to help him.

I very calmly backed the piglets into a corner. When they felt trapped with no escape, they both tried to squeeze by me at the same time. I reached down and lunged for a rear leg on each piglet. With some luck I was able to grab and hang onto each one. Soon I was hoisting up two-10# baby piglets by their rear legs.

If you have ever worked or been around pigs you know that as soon as you catch them, they immediately begin squealing in a very loud voice. And it doesn't stop until they are released. I held onto the two squealing piglets and walked up to the police captain's car. "I got them," I proclaimed. He smiled, waved me off, and rolled up his window very fast. He left very soon afterwards, I am sure to go after more dangerous criminals.

The piglets were taken to the clinic where they enjoyed a night of hospitality in one of our runs. They also made the biggest mess I have ever seen by the next morning. But luckily for us, the local humane society took them to their large animal farm, where they did eventually get adopted.

Whenever I retell this story, I really have to remind myself not to say certain things. I just cannot bring myself to tell people I saw PIGS CHASING PIGS that night. It just wouldn't be right. Or kosher.

THAT'S A BIG 10-200 GOOD BUDDY!

Our building at Gateway Pet Guardians is so large and spread out we have a walkie-talkie system for communicating with each other. It may not be the most efficient way of communicating, but it sure saves a lot of time spent walking around the building. One morning the surgery team, always the first employees into the building, was setting things up and my tech Rhianna turned on her walkie like she does every day. Apparently, our walkie system is on the same frequency as some others in the area, and since our building is located near a major highway, we occasionally hear chatter from what we assume are truckers as they pass close by. Well, this morning, just as Rhianna turned on her walkie, the following was heard. "I have got to pull over and change, man. I just pooped in my pants". That was the extent of what was said. Of course, when we all heard this, we shared a good laugh. Then I started to wonder about what the trucker could possibly be hauling cross-country. What if it was Depends? And he didn't know it.

EMPLOYEE STORIES

TO BE, OR NOT TO BE, SPAYED

Spaying female dogs or cats involves surgically removing the ovaries and uterus to prevent them from coming into heat, thereby preventing pregnancy. Neutering a male dog involves surgically removing the testicles. Both surgeries are performed to prevent certain cancers and medical conditions from developing, therefore spayed or neutered animal live longer than those dogs or cats that still have their reproductive organs intact. As the most common type of surgery performed by veterinarians, I cannot imagine how many times a day it is performed across the country and around the world. No matter how commonplace the surgeries have become, it is always important to remember the reasons why they are being done. Not just to prevent unwanted litters, but also to prolong life.

Most clients' understanding of the reasons for spaying and neutering their pets is limited to the prevention of pregnancy, and most are okay with that reasoning. Occasionally we are met with resistance from clients in the discussion of spaying or neutering their new puppy or kitten. The medical benefits are then presented and often that is enough for them to allow us to schedule the procedure. But there are still some diehards who do not want their beloved pet spayed or neutered.

Occasionally I will start to grin a little bit when I am discussing with a male client about neutering his new male puppy. Not all, but a large number of male clients are unwilling to even think about neutering their new male puppy. In the case of a reluctant male owner, if you are very observant, you may notice the very slight unintentional reflex as if I were talking about their own personal reproductive organs. It can range from a very subtle twinge of one leg in front of the other, to the overt crossing of both hands to their crotch as if I had a scalpel in my hands. This is of course an anthropomorphic imposing of human emotions on their animals. In other words, I don't want that done to me, so why should I do it to my pet.

The same reaction is usually not true when it comes to female owners and spaying their female dogs or cats. For the most part, female owners

are very understanding about the reasons for spaying or neutering their pets, and are very willing to have it done. Maybe this has something to do with that women always saying that men do not understand how hard pregnancy is because we do not have to experience the pain associated with it. No arguments from me. But I did on one occasion have to do a double take when the topic of whether to spay or not took an unexpected twist.

One of my female employees asked to speak to me in private one day. It seems that the previous night she had a nightmare which involved her coming to work and having a spay surgery performed on her that day. The nightmare was very real in her dreams and it involved her lying on the surgical table. She was obviously upset and I assured her it was just a dream and no such thing could or would ever really happen. We discussed that spaying is just a very common procedure at the clinic and it somehow came up in her subconscious. I believe that we cannot control what we dream about and I do not necessarily subscribe to the theory that our dreams are harbingers of real life events.

I was able to calm her down and we were able to get on with our day. I knew just what to say in this situation. Of course I would never spay her. She needed to think about whether she wanted to have a few litters first. And no, I did not actually say this to her.

SIZE REALLY DOES MATTER

My first clinic, City Animal Hospital, was one of, if not the first, veterinary clinic established in the city of St. Louis. It was a 1200 square foot, cement block building that was rebuilt in 1960 after the original clinic blew up due to a boiler malfunction. It consisted of a waiting room, with a very small counter for a reception desk and enough room for five to six chairs, a combination exam room/surgery room, and a small office. The back of the clinic did have quite a few kennels of varying size, because at one time boarding was a big part of the business for Dr. Schmelzer, the original owner.

At various times I made some minor changes to the building layout to increase efficiency. My father, always the handyman, built a larger reception desk and counter to accommodate our new computer system as we entered the new technology era gripping the profession. Our first computer was whale-sized to say the least and the accompanying printer was just as large. The system took up almost the entire surface of the new desk. All it did was print out reminder cards, but it was revolutionary at the time.

At the end of every appointment, we would enter client and patient information and the reminder data, which would print on postcards to be mailed the following year. I paid big bucks for a computer which did nothing to generate income until 12 months after I started using it. It did generate a lot of dust on the desk though. Interesting though, the early computer reminder system (which was fairly costly at the time) eventually morphed into one of the largest veterinary practice management systems in the world. I guess you could say I got in on the ground floor.

Besides revamping the waiting room, various times I changed other things to increase efficiency. During the free block of a veterinary student, we decided to allow her to perform surgeries in the basement while I would continue to see clients upstairs. It was a short-lived experiment as no one enjoyed transporting the animal down the stairs for surgery, and doing surgery in a basement was not ideal.

My next adventure in remodeling was to move my office downstairs into the dungeon, as we affectionately called it, and make my small office a surgical suite. "Suite" is a generous term as there was just enough room for the surgical table, anesthetic machine, my technician, and myself. Oh, and the patient of course. By this time, I had a part-time associate veterinarian and this change would allow one of us to see appointments while the other performed surgeries. While being a very small surgery suite, it did increase efficiency.

I eventually purchased the commercial property adjacent to City Animal Hospital, which consisted of a 6000 square foot building and a large parking lot. I like to think that I was farsighted in renting the building for five years. This allowed the mortgage to be paid down a lot, and allowed me plenty of time to design my dream hospital. I used to salivate thinking about moving from 1200 to 6000 square feet. I did take all of the five years to tweak my design before moving the clinic next door across the parking lot. Designing, renovating, and building out the new clinic will be another story to tell, but first I want to tell you about one of our last days in the old building.

We had by then moved our new surgery space into my old office, which was very small and cramped, but efficient. Or so we thought. The last surgery I performed in the old clinic, was on a massive Great Dane, who needed his anal sacs removed. To position the dog for this procedure we had to lay him on his chest on the table, with his hind legs hanging off of the back end, and his tail tied straight up and out of the way. The dog was so large that to accommodate him we had to turn the surgical table at an angle, from one corner of the room toward the door in the opposite corner.

After inducing anesthesia, my technician Angie was basically stuck in the opposite corner, deep in the room until I could finish. I was actually sticking out of the door frame with my instrument tray out of the room for access. I jokingly said that I do not even have to be in the same room as the patient to do surgery. Angie and I to this day laugh about our last surgery in the old building.

My architect and contractor for the renovation of the new building
used to tell me that I did not need all of the 6000 square feet available
and I should consider leasing out some of the space. All I have to do is
imagine that last surgery in the old building, where I was actually in the
hallway while my patient was in the room. "No, thank you," I would say
to their repeated attempts to lease out space in the new building. I prefer
to be in the same room as my patient to perform surgery. Besides, I think
Angie developed claustrophobia after that last surgery anyway.

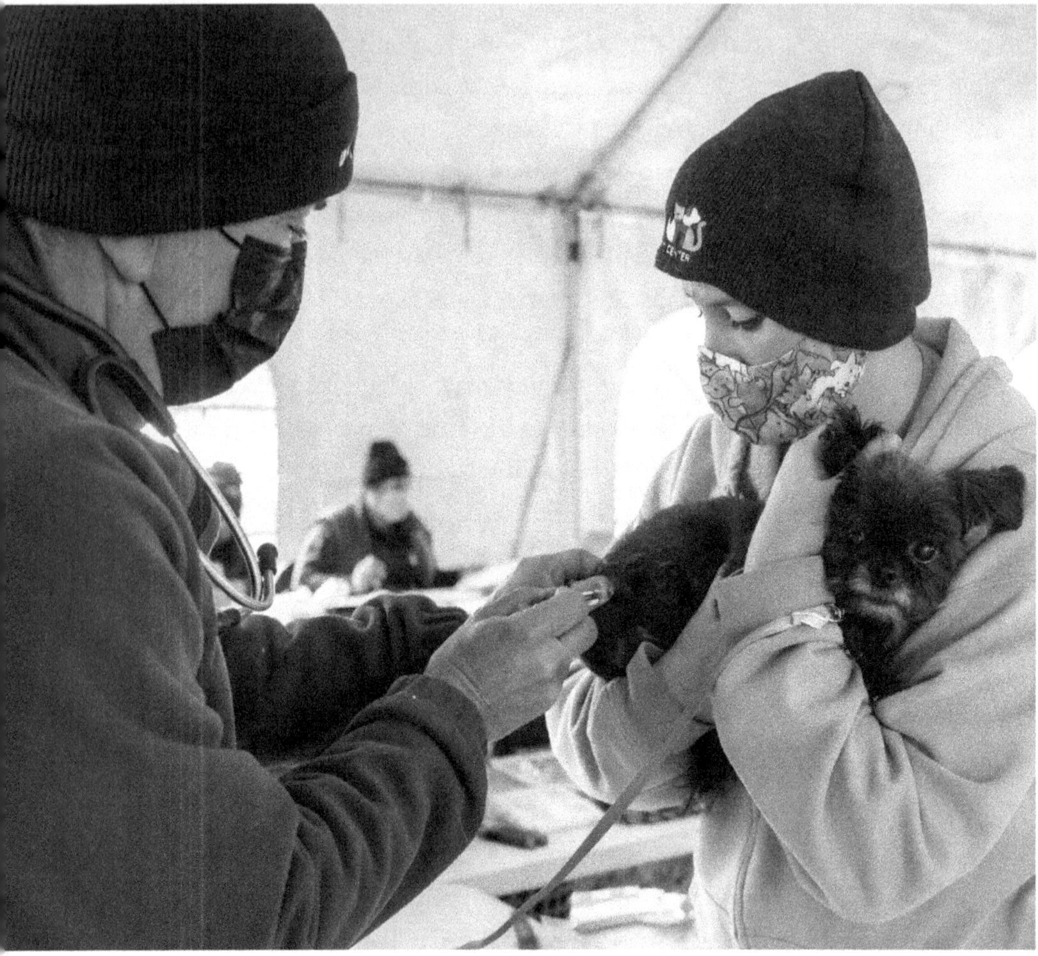

Vaccination clinic (2021)

I WANT TO ROCK AND ROLL ALL NIGHT

At Gateway Pet Guardians we commonly have to deal with litters of puppies or kittens and we will often name them all with common names of group items. Such as colors of the rainbow, ice cream brands, or in the example I am going to talk about now, rock bands. We give each member of a litter a distinctive name so the medical records can be kept accurate. Of course, once adopted, their names are more than occasionally changed by the new owners. That is of course their prerogative. One day I saw a newly adopted puppy who was part of the rock band litter. His name while part of Gateway was AC/DC. The new owner came in for an appointment for him to receive more vaccinations and to establish care at our clinic. The owner informed us that his new name was Ace. I was going to joke around the owner, and ask if they were not a fan of rock and roll music. But, instead, during the history taking part of the visit, I asked them, "How long has this been going on?". It fell on deaf ears though. Not a fan of '70s music either, I guess.

MUSINGS

URINE LUCK

Practice for me always involved fighting apathy. No matter how often you perform anesthesia, or do a spay or neuter surgery, or administer a vaccination, you must fight the sense that this is just another dull routine. Take each case seriously and never let your guard down. Never take anything for granted for sure enough that is when something will go wrong and you will make a mistake or lose a patient. For this reason, I always did more Continuing Education than required to maintain my license. I wanted to challenge myself to learn new diagnostics and new techniques, as well as keep abreast of the latest advances in the veterinary field. I always tried to equip my clinic with the best diagnostic and surgical tools, or "toys" as I like to call them. I used to joke that whoever has the most toys, wins. This is not about competition, but the incentive to use the equipment, learn more, become a better doctor, and yes, to have fun in the process.

I have always touted working with rescue organizations to my fellow veterinarians, as it affords the opportunity to try a difficult case on your own, as well as try out new techniques. While volunteering your time and expertise, you can also acquire new clients who adopted pets from these groups. But personally, the medical aspect was what gave me the most positive feedback. Most rescue organizations cannot usually afford to send difficult medical or surgical cases to a referral hospital when it is recommended. If a case is difficult to diagnose or manage in the clinic this is an option that is always offered, but the high cost of veterinary medical care can make it tough for a rescue organization to be able to afford a referral to a specialist. This is where general practitioners can step in and save the day, benefiting themselves and the rescue group.

When I first started practicing there were no specialty clinics in our area, and the only choice for referral was the university. While obviously a great choice, it was two hours away and not a viable option for most clients. If an animal needed a surgery or needed some diagnostic procedure that you had never performed before, you either figured out a way to do it or the animal did without. If it was a choice between trying

something new or the animal suffering, or worse dying, then I was up for the challenge. It afforded me the opportunity to learn new techniques and challenge my intellect and ability. Over the years I have had success stories with rescue cases that probably would not have ever had the surgery performed if I was not willing to try. And I had a few failures, but at least the animal did not suffer and was given a chance.

One rescue dog presented with bilateral inguinal hernias, in which abdominal contents squeeze through the inguinal ring in the abdomen where normally just blood vessels and nerves travel. In this case a uterine horn from each side of the abdomen had herniated out of each inguinal ring. What made this case so unique was that the dog was pregnant and a fetus was developing in each uterine horn, outside of the abdomen and just under the skin on the medial sides of both rear legs. Obviously, the dog could not successfully deliver if left to give birth. I had to perform a spay surgery by first transecting the uterine horns that were outside the body, pushing the transected uterine horns back into the abdomen through the inguinal rings, closing the hernia to prevent recurrence, and then finally entering the abdomen to finish spaying the dog. I don't remember being taught anything like this in school.

Another dog presented for what appeared to be a prolapsed vagina, where due to straining and hormonal influence, some vaginal tissue prolapsed out of its normal position. In this particular case the prolapse was unusually large. I had surgically corrected this condition on a number of occasions but was assisting my associate Betsy, so she could learn the procedure. Unfortunately, this dog was in very poor physical condition and very weak and she expired on the table during the surgery. We knew the dog was an anesthetic risk but we wanted to give her a chance. After the dog expired, we viewed the case as a teaching experience and decided to perform a necropsy to discuss the surgical technique in the event we got a similar case. I carefully incised the skin over the large swelling and it became obvious that this was not a straightforward prolapse.

During the necropsy I carefully incised around the vaginal tissue to explore the area. I was attempting to loosen the vaginal tissue, when I accidentally punctured the urinary bladder, which unbeknownst to us

was trapped in the prolapse. A tremendous spray of very foul-smelling, infected-looking urine shot out of the bladder due to pressure and showered over Betsy. This was the end of the necropsy for Betsy and the end of the teaching opportunity for me. While Betsy went to change into something drier and better smelling, I cleaned up the surgery room.

I honestly do not recall if this occurrence happened when Betsy was still a veterinary student doing a preceptorship at our clinic (she did two by the way), or if it was after I wised up and realized what an asset she would be and had hired her as an associate. As I recall the incident, it seemed I asked her to lean in to observe closely as I was dissecting tissue. It was right at that moment when I accidentally ruptured the urinary bladder sending that spray of unthinkable foulness all over her. Despite the sadness that the dog died, I actually came out of this experience smelling a lot better than Betsy did. But Betsy must really like me because she still works at Hillside, so I guess she has forgiven me.

One of my favorite veterinarians, and my good friend, Dr. Betsy Marziani

GENERATION X-GAP

When you have practiced and lived as long as I have, you experience that phenomenon known as the generation gap. I have memories of going to continuing education meetings at the beginning of my veterinary career and wondering what all the older vets were doing there. Thinking that after all of those years they must know everything and not need any further educating, I was sure they were only there socializing. Now that my friends and I are part of the older crowd, I wonder if the younger vets are thinking the same things about us. But I now know that your education never stops, and I never stop trying to better myself as a veterinarian by learning more. At the same time, this acknowledgment about veterinary education does not prevent the widening generation gap that has become evident at my clinic. As I continue to get older and my staff seemingly gets younger, I realize that I actually know less about the younger generation.

One day I came to work very excited, as I had obtained tickets for a concert that was coming to St. Louis in a few months. It was with a major musical star I was a big fan of and had seen in concert several times. I am not a big concert goer but when certain stars decide to come to St. Louis, I like to take the opportunity to see live the music that I have grown to love. I was very excited and wanted to share the good news with my staff and announced very proudly that I was going to see JT in concert when he came to St. Louis. One of my young technicians said with a straight face that she had not heard that Justin Timberlake was coming to town, nor that I was such a fan. I almost dropped my scalpel with disdain as I explained that there was only one JT, and that moniker belonged to James Taylor. The tech added insult to injury when she said she did not know who James Taylor was. Oh, this younger generation. I corrected this situation the next day when I came in with my James Taylor cassette tapes and played his music all day long. I am kidding about the cassette tapes of course, but you get the picture.

The same sort of thing happened when my friend Mark and I went to a convention. We were in the hotel bar one night, imagine that, having

drinks with some of the sales reps and other vets. As it turned out we happened to be the elder statesmen of this gathering. I don't know how this keeps happening. First the group started giving us trouble over our choice of beer, as we prefer a certain brand that is brewed in our home town of St. Louis. We were informed by the younger crowd that they considered this an "old man beer," but we just let that comment roll off of our backs as we tried to keep up with them, enjoying the "King of Beers." Then the disc jockey at the little bar played "Do You Feel Like We Do," and Mark and I exchanged high fives as we were excited to hear one of the greatest live songs from one of the greatest live albums ever. But our mood was dampened by the blank looks on the faces of the crowd we were with as they wanted to know who was singing. I replied, "You're killing me, Smalls," which was met with more blank stares as I envisioned the generation gap ever widening. Remembering that most of the crowd was probably not even born when this song and album came out, first we had to explain what an album was; then, to add insult to injury we had to explain who Peter Frampton was. Finally, I had to explain the *Sandlot* reference. You would have thought that I was speaking through a talk box or something. Oh no, not again.

In addition to music, I am a big hockey fan. My family had season tickets to the St. Louis Blues for several years and actually I had several of the players as clients. Hockey is one of the best spectator sports because of the non-stop action. The league has tried to really cater to the fans as the games have become high-tech entertainment with loud music, and fun little games during the time outs to keep the fans interested, such as Celebrity Look-alike. On the jumbotron they would pick a movie, show a picture of one of the movie's stars, and then show a live picture of someone in the crowd who that they thought looked like that celebrity. It usually brought a lot of laughs as sometimes the person live on camera would actually look like the star, or had been chosen for comic effect. Either way, the person picked to have their face on the scoreboard always seem to enjoy the attention.

One night the Celebrity Look-alike movie they picked was *SlapShot*, probably the greatest hockey movie, if not one of the greatest sports

141

movies, ever made. They showed a picture of Paul Newman from the movie, and then picked on some unsuspecting fan from the crowd, who supposedly looked like Paul Newman. This was greeted with loud cheers, at least from all of the men in the crowd. You could probably count on one hand the number of females who had ever even heard of *SlapShot*. After showing a few of the other stars in the movie and finding suitable look-alikes in the crowd, the scoreboard showed a picture of the Hanson Brothers. The crowd went crazy with raucous screaming from those who considered these three brothers to be among the greatest characters in any movie. Then the scoreboard showed a live picture of the Hanson Brothers in the crowd. They were in town for a charity event and were attending the game, even wearing their jerseys from the movie. Despite being a planned happening, it produced the loudest cheers I think I have ever heard at a hockey game.

When I got to work the next morning I was still excited about what had happened and proceeded to tell my staff that the Hanson Brothers were at the hockey game the previous night. Some of my technicians actually asked why the Hanson Brothers would be at the hockey game. It took some questions to figure out that they actually meant the band of brothers with long blond hair who had one hit song. It was all I could do to shake my head, and this time I thought about throwing my scalpel instead of just dropping it. I did not even try to explain who the REAL Hanson Brothers were, as it would fallen on deaf ears. MMM Bop, my ass. I mean, how do explain old-time hockey to a bunch of generation X-ers?

Finally, my staff surprised me one year for my birthday with tickets to see Bob Seger in concert. At least my staff knew who he was, since he has great staying power. The anticipation built slowly and the staff knew how excited I was. Finally the night of the concert arrived and it was as good as anticipated. When he starting playing one of his classics, I took out my cell phone and group texted "I think I'm going to Katmandu!!!". I immediately received messages back from two of my staff, asking, "Really, when are you going?" and the other advising, "Be careful." I think the gap just got too wide to jump.

David Backes with his silver medal from the 2010 Winter Olympic Games

WHAT'S THAT SMELL

During the course of a day at a veterinary practice it is not unusual, in fact it's fairly common, for accidents to occur and for there to be bad smells emanating from somewhere. Pets get nervous and the occasional accident will occur in the waiting room or the treatment room. A dog may express its anal sacs during an exam, and if you are really unlucky, they will get expressed on you. As this is fairly common occurrence, you will find that is why most vets and vet techs have a change of clothes handy. If nothing else there are always scrub tops and pants around to change into. If you see your veterinarian one day during an appointment wearing mis-matched scrubs, you can take it to the bank that their lab coat and nice clothes have been christened with anal sac material. There is no getting that smell out in a timely fashion. No amount of Febreeze is going to help.

I may not have the most acute sense of smell, but I do seem to be acutely sensitive to when an animal in a cage in the treatment room or in the kennels has had an accident. For one reason, I always want the clinic to smell nice when clients come in the door. As I said, accidents happen, and clients are accommodating about such things. But clients also notice when the clinic smells good and I always appreciate the comments clients make about such. The first impressions made by a client when they come into the clinic for the first time are so important and that is why we always strived to have a very clean, and clean-smelling, clinic.

Sometimes just walking by reveals who the offending animal is, but sometimes the "accident" may be hidden under a blanket or towel or even under the animal. Then a little detective work is needed to clean up the situation and/or the animal, as we want keep the clinic inviting, but also strive to make the animals comfortable.

One day, I kept getting a whiff of fecal material, was not an overwhelming odor, but none the less it was recurrent. There did not seem to be a pattern or area where it was the worst. I did my usual detective work and checked all the cages, and litter boxes, but all were clean. I even checked the trash cans around the clinic but could not surmise

the source of the odor. It was not the lab area where fecal samples are checked. I even asked my staff about the odor, and everyone took a turn looking around but we could not locate the source of the smell.

I was in the pharmacy area filling a prescription when I noticed the smell again, just a faint whiff of fecal material, at the moment when one of my staff happened to be walking by. I immediately asked her if she smelled anything, but she commented that she had a bit of a head cold and was congested and could not smell anything too well that day. As I was talking to her I noticed the smell again and it seemed to be emanating from her direction.

Not wanting to embarrass her I asked again if she smelled anything. She looked a little puzzled but then did admit that now that she had stopped walking she did detect a faint fecal smell. We came to the conclusion that it was coming from her, and although she checked her scrub top and did not notice any stains, when she checked her front pocket of her top, she found a small fecal ball there. She came to the conclusion that a short while earlier, while she had been carrying a cute little puppy around showing it off to everyone, the puppy had an accident. She thought the feces had just fallen on the floor, but at least one must have fallen into her pocket. Having a cold she did not smell it and had been walking around for a couple of hours with some fecal material in her pocket.

We did not want to embarrass her too much but of course there was some good natured kidding that went on after the discovery. Someone pulled out the old standard, "He who smelt it dealt it" line. I was reminded of the song by The Pretenders, "Brass in Pocket." With a twist, of course. Everyone at the clinic is very close and naturally we had some fun at her expense. But we were not too tough on her though as we are respectful of people's feelings. We would never want to be the cause of someone feeling worse than she did already. After all, she was having a pretty shitty day.

THE GROSSEST OF THE GROSS

As a young veterinarian, I used to believe getting urinated on was the worst thing that could happen to me over the course of a day. Oh, how wrong I was about that. Sure enough came the day a puppy with parvo squirted bloody diarrhea on my new shoes. Shortly afterward, when I was sure that being defecated on was the worst thing that could happen to me on the job, once again, I was proven wrong. Then, after anal sac material was expressed onto my clothes, I was sure that had to be the worst occurrence of them all. But then, just like that, anal sac material was splattered all over my face, and my convictions didn't hold up to the test of "real life" veterinary medicine.

Now that I've set a pleasant scene, I want to tell you a story about the grossest thing I've had the "pleasure" of witnessing in all my years of practicing veterinary medicine. But first, I should give you a little background information. Veterinarians have the strongest stomachs of any people I've ever encountered. Among the group of vets I get together with for lunch on a monthly basis, nothing is off-limits during our meal-time discussions. Why, we've been known to drive off diners at neighboring tables with our discussions of cat bite abscesses with green pus, draining tracts, explosive bloody diarrhea, and ghastly smells. All the while, we never stop enjoying our tomato soup or nachos with guacamole dip.

I have no problem treating tedious cases; however, I'm not immune from getting the "willies" on occasion. There is one situation or diagnosis that to this day is my worst nightmare. That one word is myiasis. Oh sorry, for you laypeople that word means maggots. You see, flies have an innate way of speedily laying eggs inside fresh open wounds. Their young, known as maggots, hatch within hours and have a nice warm place to develop. Every year, a dog or cat is brought into the clinic with a maggot-infested open wound. There's something about seeing those things crawling under an animal's skin that makes my own skin crawl.

Recently we had a volunteer from the dog rescue group bring in a stray dog she'd picked up laying near the side of the road. The dog was so weak, it didn't even object to being picked up, and the volunteer at first thought it might be dead. It was rushed to the clinic, and not long after being examined, it became immediately obvious why it was so weak. The dog had multiple large open wounds on the top of its head, stretching from one ear to the other and down its neck towards its chest. Crawling around in the wounds were literally thousands of maggots. They were also found in and around the ear canals and in wounds on all four legs. While the staff and I were very repulsed and fought back some nausea, we were also driven to help the dog.

I quickly assessed the dog's condition and administered a sedative and an analgesic to address the dog's pain and to allow us to start the cleanup. While I went to check on another appointment, my technicians went to work cleaning up the dog. As soon as they tried to clip off some of the hair, the dog shook his head violently. Maggots, tissue fluid, and who knows what else, went flying everywhere. One of my poor technicians, Angie, got hit square in the face with all of this "stuff" and immediately passed out backward on the floor. Everyone screamed and I came running immediately. My first concern was for my poor technician. I got a towel for her head, then a wet washcloth to wipe off her face. For her part, Angie remembers waking up and seeing my mom standing over her, looking down and calling her name. Angie assured us she was fine, and was able to sit up in a minute or two, so I went back to helping out the dog.

Later, I suggested my technician should take the rest of the day off, but to her credit she insisted on staying. It took us an hour, or more, to clean up the treatment area. There were maggots and blood everywhere... even inside one of our cabinets that happened to be open at the wrong time. On the countertop was a small open container of chlorhexidine cream, which we were using to treat the dog's wounds when the shaking occurred. Yes, you guessed it. There were flies in the ointment.

A LITTLE DAB WILL DO YA

One of our rescue dogs came back from its foster parents and unfortunately, we decided that it was not being cared for properly. It had lost more than 12 pounds, with no medical reason to explain this weight loss. The dog also was extremely dirty and just generally did not look like it had been cared for at all. We took the dog back under the explanation that we needed to explore its weight loss, with the real reason being that we needed to get it out of that foster home.

After a thorough physical examination and some laboratory work, we decided to give the dog a bath. Two of my assistants put the dog in the tub and washed off what seemed like a year's worth of dirt and grime. It seemed to be taking them a long time in the grooming room, so I went back to investigate.

The assistants informed me that after bathing the dog, they had put on a coat conditioner. It was a free sample of a new product, something that guaranteed a brighter, shinier coat. But the techs were finding it very difficult to wash off of the dog's fur. They had been rinsing the dog for about ten minutes when I popped in. It seemed that no matter how much they rinsed, the conditioner just would not come off so well.

I looked at the bottle and tried to control my laughter. I explained to the girls that their theory was right, but their application was all wrong. This product works from the inside out, not from the outside in. You see, they had been applying a dietary supplement, meant to be added to the dog's food, to the dog's fur instead.

After a bit more scrubbing the dog looked a lot better. The dog even ate some of the conditioner when we applied it to her food later. I asked the techs, "Now, wasn't that easier?"

HELP! I'VE VOMITED AND I CAN'T GET UP!

During our Minor Medical Clinic at Gateway Pet Guardians, where clients are seen on a first-come, first-served, basis, a client drove up and called our phone line to announce they were in the parking lot. She told us she had called 911 and they had told her to come to our clinic immediately. Thinking that perhaps there was a real emergency, we went out to the parking lot and asked her to fill out some paperwork, and we made preparations to see her pet right away. But she informed us that she had no money for the exam fee that day. So, we questioned her on what had prompted her call to 911 that day. She said her cat had vomited once. After she had fed the cat 10 cat treats. I sure hope the 911 operator appreciated the gravity of the situation. Think how flooded the 911 lines would be if everyone called because their cat vomited. Once.

MUSINGS

LONG-DISTANCE RELATIONSHIP

"Back away from the dog, Vince," I scolded my young veterinary assistant. He had come into the exam room and immediately knelt down to pet the dog. I think his head was in the clouds, believing veterinary medicine was all about taking care of dogs who just wanted to lick your face. He had yet to be brought back down to earth by suffering a dog bite, and I couldn't allow him to get bitten on my watch if I could help it. I've always been more worried about my staff getting bitten than myself.

Before I entered the exam room, I noticed a large red CAUTION sticker affixed to the top of this dog's chart. I scanned the chart and it all came back to me. My associate veterinarian, Dr. Micah Young, had seen this dog just a few weeks before for a skin infection. This particular dog, a rescue, was one of those dogs that'd lash out in fear, not out of meanness. Knowing this didn't make working on the dog easier, but it helped validate its source of aggression.

Just to fully examine this fearful dog's skin required sedation. It was no small feat to get the sedative injected into the dog's rear leg. Such situations reinforce the importance of staff safety when it comes to working with stray and feral dogs. Once the dog was asleep, we could examine it easily and without fear of being attacked. It was a win-win solution because once the dog was sedated, there was nothing for it to fear as well.

But that was then, and this is now. The foster parent brought the dog back in for a recheck examination and noted that the dog was still a little too itchy. When I entered the exam room, I was immediately greeted by a not-so-low growl from a dog sitting with its back against the far-right corner. As I stepped further into the room, the growl became a full-fledged bark of warning. Even if Vince didn't, I knew not to go any closer.

I tried to elicit as much information as I could from the foster parent about how the dog was doing. I kept sneaking glances, without making eye contact, while the dog moved around the room. The skin sure looked good from where I was standing. I was thinking, "There was really no need to approach the dog, was there?" And I happened to like my hands and fingers the way they were. I'd need them for the next appointment anyway.

The foster parent assessed the situation and decided that the dog need-ed to know I indeed wasn't a threat. She decided to prove it by having me come around the exam table so we could make a show of shaking hands. She did so emphatically, while telling the dog what a great doctor I was. Imagine the picture if you can: There I was, trying to keep an eye on the dog in the corner while some over-enthusiastic foster parent is saying, "Good doctor, he is our friend. Just ignore those needles he is holding in his other hand. He's our friend and we like him." And to top it all off, I was instructed to smile at the dog.

It may have been my imagination, but it seemed like the dog relaxed a little bit as our play-acting went on. Mind you, it wasn't enough for me to want to go over and let him lick my face. At one point, he turned his head to the side and got a sort of quizzical look on his face, which made me wonder exactly what he was thinking about all of this. Did he think that maybe I wasn't a threat after all? Or was he wondering why I never received a biscuit from his caregiver after shaking hands? After all, he always did.

WORDS WITH FRIENDS

Our clinic is a completely paperless practice, at which the receptionists are responsible for booking most of our appointments, adding them to the appropriate day's schedule. Of course, whoever happens to take a phone call for an appointment request can do it also. When a call comes in requesting an appointment, it is added to the schedule and color-coded as a Routine Wellness exam, such as for vaccinations and such, or as a Medical Examination for a sick animal, etc. There may also be some small notes entered in the computer at the time of the booking of the appointment to help the staff and doctor know in advance what is needed for that particular visit, or so you would think.

During appointments, the veterinary technicians are charged with obtaining a history from the clients, which is the subjective reason why the animal is presented to the clinic. For an Annual Wellness Examination, clients are asked how the pets are doing, are they eating and drinking normally, and if there are any concerns about the pet. If it is a Medical Examination appointment, the history may be a little bit more involved, as the technician's questions can help the doctor to determine what is wrong. The techs are very good at not only entering the notes into the computer, but also for telling the doctor a quick synopsis before we enter the exam room together.

Once I had an appointment to see a sick cat and I read in the history notes "cat has an automatic fever." All kinds of thoughts were going through my mind as I entered the room. Dogs and cats can occasionally have relapsing fevers, where their body temperature can fluctuate, in and out of normal range, due to various conditions. Could this be one of those rare conditions? Could it be that this was going to be one of my favorite pastimes in veterinary medicine, the zebra hunt?

There is a saying in veterinary medicine that goes, "When you hear hoof beats, think horses, not zebras". What this means is that it is much more common to find a reasonable explanation for an animal's clinical signs, then a rare explanation. A famous veterinary clinician, who had a

list of adages made up to help out all of us frustrated veterinarians, once said, "It is much more expected to find a rare manifestation of a common illness, rather than a common occurrence of a rare illness". I know that I have paraphrased his exact quote but the point is still the same. Think horses, not zebras.

Although one of my favorite pastimes is the zebra hunt, I soon realized that I would have to take off my pith helmet, change out of my safari hunting clothes, and put my white exam coat back on. It seems my tech had meant to say "automatic feeder" instead of "automatic fever." This part of the pet's nutrition history was important in helping us get to the bottom of what was wrong, but it meant there would be no zebra hunt that day.

One particular day I noticed that one of the rescue dogs we had seen in the past was coming in for a recheck. The notes under this appointment read, "Dog coming in for a DNA swap." I seem to have a knack at being able to read between the lines, and knowing what my staff usually means, instead of what they are actually saying. But in this case, I was not quite so confident. Occasionally a client will describe me as being a magician when it comes to caring for their pets, and I have been known to pull the proverbial rabbit out of a diagnostic hat. I am not bragging here, but rather I am actually admitting that I have gotten lucky on numerous occasions. I like to say that sometimes the patients get better in spite of us, not because of us. But I am not a genetic magician by any means.

Well, getting back to the dog in question, he was actually here today to have a DNA test done. The owners were interested in determining his breed, and these tests have become quite in vogue recently. I usually tell clients that while they can be fun, the test results would not hold up in court. This is not CSI Hillside here, and when an 80# dog comes back with some Chihuahua genes, you can't help but have to shake your head. Really? I do not want the image of that breeding in my head. The notes for the appointment should have been "DNA swab, not a DNA swap."

Sometimes owners will want us to fudge the breed listing of their dog in our medical records. In this day and age of breed restrictions, landlords or insurance companies will sometimes not allow for certain breeds, such as Pit Bulls, Rottweilers, etc. We try to work with the clients if there is some wiggle room on what breed a dog actually could be, but we will not lie on any kind of official form as our license could be at stake.

But then I started to think if we could somehow alter the DNA of a dog, and have it hold up in court, we could open up a whole new revenue stream for the clinic." I swear Judge Judy, he's not a Pit Bull, he's a Dachshund."

THAT'S A BAD OMEN.

As you drive east about 40 miles out of St. Louis on Highway 64 there is a town called Damiansville. I have passed it multiple times on my travels east. I always liked the name of the town, but it struck me as an odd name. Something about it tugged at the back of my brain every time I saw the exit sign. Who is this guy Damian and how did he come to have a town named after him? Then I remembered that one of my clients had mentioned it. They had traveled there to pick up their new puppy. It seems there is a breeder of Rottweilers there who produces great guard dogs. Oh yeah, the exit for Damiansville is #666.

My daughter Nina trying on David Backes' silver medal, with my daughter Anna

EMPLOYEE STORIES

TRICK OR TREAT

Since I was a kid, I have always enjoyed Halloween. As a kid it was about getting the maximum amount of candy and then getting sick from over-eating it after trick or treating. As an adult I can admit to still craving the candy, but as I have gotten older the holiday has become more about the costumes. Not just any costume will do, mind you. I have begun to go for the "play on words" costumes, or the ones that make you think about the meaning of the costume. It's all in line with the stupid dad joke façade I struggle so hard to maintain.

At the clinic one year I took an old scrub shirt and stapled pictures of different types of cars all over it. It was a fairly unpretentious and low-key costume, but I did have all of my staff and my clients stumped. I had offered a small cash prize to any of my staff who could figure it out, but I was able to keep my wallet closed all day. Have you figured out what I was? I was a Car-Vet. Get it? I can hear the groans from here.

Another year I went to a florist supply store and purchased some fake grass. The grass was about six inches tall and in large squares, which I cut and applied to the top of my surgical cap and to the back of another old scrub top. Once again I offered a cash reward for anyone who could figure out my costume. Once again, I prevailed. Any takers? I was a Chia-Vet. Okay, okay, I know how corny it was but give me some credit for imagination.

I got an idea for a recent costume while out shopping. I was in my scrubs, I had just gotten off work, and stopped at the store to pick something up. As I was checking out, the cashier asked if I was a doctor. I said I was and she asked me where I worked. Trying to be funny I pointed to the DVM insignia on my scrub top and said that I worked for the Department of Motor Vehicles. She smiled and said that I must be the doctor giving the eye exams. I did let her in on my attempted joke and then got to work on the costume. On my scrub top I changed the "DVM" to "DMV," attached copies of several driver's licenses, put a picture that said "Now Serving," with a number flashing on my surgical cap, and had

a ticket stub coming out of my breast pocket that said "Take a Number."
Not everyone got my joke, or those that did just shook their head at me.

Several years ago, Halloween happened to fall on my scheduled day
off, so I was not going into work, and therefore not dressing up. Some-
time around mid-morning I received a call from the clinic asking me to
come in to deal with some problem that apparently only I could handle.
This would happen rather often, so I was not suspicious about the call at
all. But when I got to the clinic, I was met with a big surprise.

Every single one of my staff had dressed up as "Dr. Ed" for Halloween.
There were young versions from pictures of me early in my career and
older versions of me as I look today. A couple staff members were wearing bright fluorescent workout clothes I favor, and several soccer jerseys
were in the bunch. One staff member dressed up like a cat to mimic
my cat, Coal. And of course, everyone, including all of the ladies, had
painted on mustaches and goatees in my likeness. It is one of my favorite
Halloween memories as the photos illustrate. They say imitation is the
sincerest form of flattery. Well, that day I was beyond flattered. My staff
never looked better, in my opinion.

Dr. Ed Look-alike Day at Hillside Animal Hospital

THE WORLD IS GOING TO THE BIRDS

As you can probably tell from reading some of my stories, I love movies. I love to be entertained for a couple of hours and losing myself in the story line. Among my favorites are all of Alfred Hitchcock's works, and one of the best is *The Birds*. I admit that did freak me out a bit when I was younger, but as I grew older I began to appreciate the cinematic greatness it represents. Before telling you a story associated with this movie, I would like to share my experiences working with birds.

In veterinary school I was fortunate to go to Las Vegas for a clinical block rotation and work with a veterinarian named Gary Weddle. He allowed me to stay at his house for two months while working at his clinic. His house had a large pool with a spa attached, and was home to two large cockatoos, an iguana, and a horse. Gary actually went on vacation while I was there and I was left in charge of the house and pet care. I bonded early on with the two birds, and it was not uncommon to allow them out of the cage to walk around the living room while watching TV or relaxing. The birds took to me and would climb all over me, never biting me once, which Gary said was unusual for them. This was my first experience with large birds, and I was at first a little nervous but then began to enjoy them.

Gary, who did a lot of exotic animal work, was called out for a house call one day and I got to tag along. We went to Wayne Newton's home to take care of his penguins. Yes, you read that right, penguins in Las Vegas. Alas, I did not get to meet the great singer, but I did get a glimpse of the lifestyles of the rich and famous. I probably would have embarrassed myself by asking him to sing "Danke Schoen." I know, another movie reference. *Ferris Bueller's Day Off* for those scratching their heads.

Gary had a ring-necked parakeet at the clinic which sat in a large cage behind the reception desk. These large parakeets, about the size of a small parrot, have bright green feathers and a characteristic ring of orange around their necks, hence the name. I cannot remember the bird's name, but it had quite a vocabulary and would talk to the clients check-

ing in or checking out. Its favorite thing to say was, "Pay your bill," to the clients at the desk. As a parting gift to Gary, I tried repeatedly to get the bird to say "Gaaaary," drawing out his name in that nasally parakeet voice. The staff thought it was hilarious, but I was gone before I heard what the boss thought about this.

Gary took me to the bird breeder and gifted me the same kind of parakeet to take home. I named him Rocky, and he traveled by car with me back home and eventually became a mascot at the clinic. Rocky learned a few words, mostly his name, but did enjoy screeching at the top of his lungs at the dogs and cats coming into the exam room. He lived at the clinic for many years before I decided he would be happier living with other birds, and one of our clients adopted him

One day while living in the clinic, he was sitting on top of his cage as I cleaned it out. I had his wings clipped but he could still fly a little bit. Right then my father came into the clinic through the side door and Rocky made a mad dash for freedom. I immediately ran out after him but there was no sight of him. Then all of a sudden, he flew from over my head, across the busy street in front of the clinic, during rush hour traffic. I dodged cars and risked my life to chase after him. He then crossed two sets of railroad tracks which thankfully were not in use at that moment. Remember, his wing feathers had been clipped and he could not fly that well, otherwise he would have been long gone. Living most of his life in a cage, he did not have much stamina. With me in pursuit, he proceeded to fly directly into a large brick wall of a building across the street, and fell to the ground. I raced over, picked him up, wrapped him in a towel I had grabbed, and brought the stunned bird to safety. His short sojourn of freedom was frantic but unrewarding. He was not in a hurry to leave the safety of the clinic after that, but his misadventure did remind me of another stupid dad joke. " What did the bird say that flew into the concrete wall?" "Dam."

During the early years of my veterinary career, I did some volunteer veterinary work for The World Bird Sanctuary (WBS), a wonderful organization dedicated to helping mainly injured raptors and birds of prey. I

will never call myself an avian vet, but I was able to provide some basic veterinary care for these magnificent specimens. It was always a fun day at the clinic when the volunteers from the WBS would bring over some carriers and then take out a bald eagle or golden eagle, or some kind of hawk for us to work on. After some years the organization did find some vets with more bird experience, and that was okay with me. But whenever I go to a baseball game, and the WBS is there to do an eagle fly over (releasing a trained bald eagle from center field bleachers to fly down to the infield and its awaiting trainer), I remember my earlier work and think that in some small part I helped out the organization, if not that particular bird.

I have a good friend from vet school, Dr. EJ Ehrhart, who graduated a year behind me. He is now a veterinary pathologist living in Colorado. We are still good friends but do not get to see each other enough. EJ had a love for birds and assisted me at the WBS several times, giving me tips for working on them. After graduating, EJ lived back in St. Louis for a time. He had a small parrot as a pet but no one to care for the bird while he was going to be away. He finally asked his mom and dad if they could take care of the bird.

Unfortunately, his mom was one of those people with a tremendous fear of birds and told him in no uncertain terms that she would not have anything to do with it. Therefore, it was up to EJ's father to care for the bird. Everyone agreed and EJ went on vacation. Well, picture this scene if you can. EJ's mom came home one day from shopping, came in the kitchen door, put down the groceries, and noticed that the door to the large bird cage had somehow been left open and that the bird was not in the cage. Her fear of birds was so great that she grabbed a towel, threw it over her head, stood in a corner of the kitchen, and began screaming for help.

Hearing her recount the story after the fact, I found it impossible not to laugh about it. If you are not one of the people with that fear, ornithophobia by the way, I guess it is difficult to relate. She did calm down a

little bit, but then got scared even more when she looked down towards the floor from under the towel, and saw the parrot, looking up at her, tilting its head and saying 'Hello." I am sure the bird was wondering what all the fuss was about.

Finally, I am coming to the part about The *Birds* movie I mentioned earlier. My friend, client, and former employee Janet, is married to Eric and they are one of the most fun couples I have had the privilege to know. Besides their multiple dogs and cats, they had a large parrot which had the most incredible vocabulary. And a great sense of humor to go along with it. The bird loved to make fun of the other pets and its owners. He would call out to the dog in a loud voice, "Sammy, go outside?" Of course, Sammy would get all excited, head to the back door, and then the bird would start to laugh out loud. He never got tired of doing this, and unfortunately Sammy was a slow learner.

The bird also learned to imitate Janet and Eric's voices pretty well. If the phone would ring, the bird would say in Janet's voice, "Eric, it's your mom." It would also imitate a conversation that must have taken place enough times for the bird to hear it and repeat it back. In Eric's voice the bird would call out "Honey Ham!" to Janet, and then immediately the bird would scream back, "What?" in Janet's voice. "Honey Ham!" "What?"

Janet and Eric went to a Halloween party one year in a tuxedo and fancy dress, wearing makeup up to make it look like they had been attacked by *The Birds*. Their fake injuries, included an eye out, scratches, birds in their hair, and lots of fake blood and bird poop on their clothes. They looked fantastic and of course won the best costume award. They are such a fun couple and I miss seeing them a lot.

Well, I hope you enjoyed my life experiences with birds. My life may not be going to the birds, but it has been a flight of fancy for me.

RESCUE ME

THERE'S PUPPY MILLS
IN THEM THERE HILLS

I first started working with Randy Grim before he created Stray Rescue of St. Louis. He was rescuing dogs and cats on his own, while spending his own money or begging for help from his friends. He's saved hundreds of animals from life, and probable death, on the streets and we were happy to help him out with this huge effort. It wasn't long after forming our relationship that we went on one of our first adventures.

One day Randy received a phone call from a woman in south-central, rural Missouri. She owned a trailer park, had a serious problem, and no one was willing to help her. Tenants in the trailer park that she owned were running a small breeding operation out of their trailer. After falling behind on the rent, they picked up and left one night leaving all of the dogs and cats behind. The trailer park owner unsuccessfully tried to get local law enforcement and animal control officers to help, but to no avail.

It had been over two weeks that the animals had been abandoned and no help could be found. The trailer park owner, to her credit, was trying her best to feed all of the animals, but she was very overwhelmed. She broadened her search for help to the St. Louis area and eventually found her way to Randy, who agreed to assist. And of course, I couldn't say no to Randy when he asked for my help.

So, one Saturday, after we finished appointments, a caravan consisting of myself, my Veterinary Technician Carrie, Randy, and his VW van along with two friends, and a television crew from a local station all made the two-hour drive to this trailer park. I packed my truck with any supplies I thought we might need and as many crates as we could carry. It was a long ride and we had no idea what to expect when we got there.

Nothing could have prepared us for what we found. This was a day that we'd never forget. When we arrived, the trailer park owner greeted us, surrounded by a pack of beagles and mixed- breed dogs numbering at least 15. They all looked alright at first glance, but when we saw where they came from, it was amazing they looked as good as they did...and

especially amazing that they were as happy as they were.

The owner took us to the trailer from which she had rescued all of these dogs, which looked as if it could fall apart at any moment. Attached to the side was a homemade cage made of two-by -fours and chicken wire. It was about one foot wide and two feet deep. The bottom of the cage was covered with six inches of fecal material. The owner of the trailer park told us that the cage contained five cats before she'd released them. It was the first time I'd seen anything like this.

All of the windows in the trailer were either broken or had screens torn out. When we walked inside, we found out why. Several of us almost got physically sick from the smell we encountered. The stench was an overpowering combination of fecal and urine smell. The floors of the trailer were covered with a thick layer of fecal material. There was evidence of where the dogs had been tied or chained to the walls of the trailer, and where the dogs had chewed or scratched the walls and window sills in an attempt to escape. The bathroom was almost unrecognizable in its condition. There was no talking as we walked through the trailer, but there was some retching, some gasps, and a lot of sobs as we were otherwise stunned into silence as we thought about what it must have been like to be trapped in this hellhole.

The television crew took lots of footage of these terrible conditions, and then took footage of the dogs and cats. They also filmed us loading all of the dogs and cats into crates and then into the vehicles. They then took off to get home and hopefully get what was possibly some of the first footage of a puppy mill rescue ever seen on the news, as this was many years before the issue was a hot topic.

After loading up, we took off on the two-hour ride back to St. Louis. Someone had the bright idea to go home a different way, hoping it would be a little shorter. Taking the back roads, we stopped at a gas station in a very small town to try and clean up a little bit. Then Randy's VW bus would not start, which apparently was a common issue with his vehicle. I only wish that I'd known this before being broken down in rural Missouri. We could see several men inside the gas station, but they did not seem to have any interest in helping. For all I know one of them could

have been the tenant of the trailer we just left. I told Carrie to roll down the window and listen for banjos as we push-started the VW.

After a long drive, we made it back to St. Louis and the clinic. On a sad note, a little beagle who looked okay when we left the trailer park had died during the trip. An autopsy revealed that she was heartworm positive and this most likely contributed to her sudden death. It took another couple of hours to check out the rest of the animals and get them settled into nice warm cages with soft bedding. The rest of the dogs were also heartworm positive and all had intestinal and skin parasites. All in all, it was a very long day but we were successful in rescuing 20 animals from a horrible existence. One of the beagles was pregnant and was fostered by one of my employees, Jan. Another one of the beagles was a young male, and Carrie decided to adopt him. He ended up living a very long and fulfilling life after his rough start.

The film crew was successful in getting the report on the evening news and it generated some good publicity for Randy and his rescue efforts. The feed even made it onto the national news a few days later. Not long after, Randy was contacted by a director of a show that aired on Animal Planet. Another crew came to interview us and film the rescued animals, even going to Jan's house to visit the pregnant beagle. A few weeks later, I videotaped the newborn beagle pups and continued to tape them several more times as they grew up.

The original news footage, along with the interviews done in St. Louis, and even some of my amateur videotape footage, all made it onto a show called, of all things, *Wild Animal Rescues,* on Animal Planet. It was one of those shows that would be rerun often. Over the following years, I'd often get a call from a long-lost friend or classmate saying they'd been channel surfing late at night and happened upon me on Animal Planet. I never knew when the episode was airing but this type of phone call was repeated at least 10 times over a several years. Most of my friends wanted to know what kind of veterinary practice I was in to be included in an episode of *Wild Animal Rescues.* I always tell them that most of my life at the clinic is normal, but I still occasionally will have some days that could be considered for another episode.

Community outreach for Gateway Pet Guardians (2019)

MONSTER QUEST?

Through my work with Stray Rescue and other groups, I've been interviewed on the news concerning animal welfare issues and various rescues. I've also had the opportunity to be involved in several unusual television segments that can still be found on the web. Each episode aired on not-so-typical animal shows. The first was on a show called *Wild Animal Rescues* and the second was on a show called, of all things, *Monster Quest*. Over the years the two episodes will sporadically be rerun on late night, but I never know when that is going to happen. Very recently while trying to finish this book, I received a text from a classmate and friend who I had not talked to for at least 3 years. His cryptic text just said, "Have you caught the monster yet?" I knew immediately that the episode must have aired again.

Monster Quest features episodes of people in search of the Loch Ness Monster, Bigfoot, and other "mythical," rarely seen and never-captured creatures. For this particular episode, we were in search of the often seen, yet seldom captured, stray feral dog. At the time of the taping, we all were trying to help solve the problem of the packs of feral dogs that were common in East St. Louis, IL. I had teamed up with Stray Rescue and some researchers from the University of Missouri to see where dogs in a certain area traveled during the day and night, in pursuit of their normal behavior.

The researchers from the University had a camera, which had originally been used on deer in a wildlife setting, retrofitted to a dog collar. I guess you could say it was the precursor to the GoPro. If I had any foresight, I should have marketed it as the Canine GoPro. Oh well, another money-making idea thought about too late. This camera would record for a six-to eight-hour period and was designed with GPS tracking through a radio transmitter emitting a signal to a laptop computer. When another signal was sent to the collar, it would fall off of the dog, then we could use the GPS to find where it lay. It all sounded fine in theory.

My involvement included checking out the dog in question. All involved, including Randy from Stray Rescue, the researchers, the crew

from *Monster Quest*, myself, and my technician went over to an area in East St. Louis, IL, known for feral dogs, and set up a live trap to capture one. We baited the trap with food, and stepped away. It didn't take long for us to catch a scared, stray female dog. Then it was my turn for action. With some help, I was able to inject her with a sedative so we could safely work on her with as little stress as possible. After she was asleep, I performed a quick physical exam, took some samples for parasite testing, and vaccinated her. Then the researchers put on the collar, tested to make sure it worked, and began taping. I administered a reversal agent for the sedative and after a few minutes, the dog woke up, got to her feet, and ran away to join her pack.

The researchers had the radio collar tracking on their laptop using an antenna to follow where the dog was going. She ended up in a wooded area not too far from where we started. We found a bunch of trails and followed them as best we could. The radio collar signal told us the general direction that the dog was traveling, and if we were getting closer or farther away. It was a very cold day, but we kept warm by running several miles in pursuit of the dog. We tracked her for a couple of hours before eventually losing the signal, then packed it in for a couple of hours to allow the dog to settle down, hoping to review her daily routine on the camera footage later.

After a designated amount of time, the researchers attempted to activate the mechanism that caused the collar to drop off. Unfortunately, it did not work as planned and they could tell from the signal that it was still attached to the dog and moving. It was at this point that we thought the day was going to be a total loss. The dog, the camera, and the video in the camera seemed to be gone forever.

The next day Randy and the television crew went back to the same location to scout things out. They could see some of the same dog pack hanging around. As it was winter and very cold, when Randy put out some food, more dogs started to come around. The crew took a chance, set up the live trap, and stepped back again. A short while later, they could see that the trapping had been successful in catching a dog, and would you believe, it was the same dog with the collar still on her. It was,

169

to say the least, a miracle that we caught the same dog twice.

The dog was transported in the live trap to the clinic. Once at the clinic, we were able to retrieve the dog's collar. The researchers went to work analyzing the video, while we went to work on the dog. I am happy to say that we went on to have her spayed and she eventually was adopted into a forever home.

At first the computer card used in the camera was corrupted, and the film data unreadable. I asked my friend Brian Ward, my local computer expert, for his help in recovering the footage if possible. Brian and his team at Lazerware worked their magic and recovered all of the footage from the camera from the previous 24 hours. One of his employees, Paul, even received credit during the show's airing for his efforts.

The video obtained from the dog was pretty amazing. It was like watching the jumpy style of *The Blair Witch Project*, with the dog running through the woods on the same trails we had tried to follow. It also showed the dog and her fellow pack members entering an abandoned house and looking around. At one point, another dog was sniffing and looking at the strange collar, and even trying to pull it off the dog. Talk about extreme close-up. All in all, it was a very fascinating video to watch and we learned a little bit about feral dog behavior.

The episode of *Monster Quest* aired and we had a party to watch it. The producers put together all of the videos, from the initial trapping to the video from the dog, and even included the second trapping and the work we did at the clinic. The episode was seen by a lot of people and once again, I received calls from people I had not talked to in forever. There was quite a stretch of time when I had not heard any more about the show, until just a few weeks prior to finishing the book. The conversation with my friend brought back a flood of memories. I can't say we actually found any monsters on the show, but we did embark on one great quest.

My daughter Nina and I on community outreach for Gateway Pet Guardians

RESCUE ME

PLAY BALL

For decades, baseball has been tightly woven into our nation's fabric. Nowhere is this truer than in St. Louis. The love affair between the St. Louis Cardinals and their fans is unrivaled in any other city. I often hear other team's announcers talk about the support that the Cardinals receive from their fans; how much Cardinal fans appreciate good plays even made by the other team; and how other teams love to come to St. Louis and play in this uplifting atmosphere. An important part of that love affair between St. Louis fans and the Cardinals involved the former manager, Tony LaRussa.

Not everyone may agree with my assessment, however. Those who love Tony LaRussa think he might have been the greatest mind in baseball. Those who don't, think he's arrogant. I think both groups would agree on one thing: Tony's love of animals is a well-known fact, evidenced by his Animal Rescue Foundation and the great work they do for animal welfare.

A particular rescue case I was involved with that not only tugged at our hearts but apparently Tony LaRussa's as well. A dog rescued and brought to the clinic by Stray Rescue of St. Louis was found to have some horrible injuries. The skin on the dog's face and head had been burned, and all that was left was raw, inflamed flesh. The entire cartilaginous tip of his nose had been burned away. He looked horrible and was in obvious pain. We started treatment for shock and pain and immediately addressed the wounds. Upon closer inspection, we determined that the particular type of burn wounds the dog had suffered was likely caused by acid thrown on the dog. We could not conceive of any natural occurrence or exposure that would have caused this.

We were able to stabilize the dog which was in unbelievably good spirits despite his horrible wounds. Stray Rescue named the dog Rick, and he ended up spending a couple of days at our clinic. Eventually, he was transferred to a local veterinary specialty practice where the veterinary surgeons performed some incredible plastic surgery, including rebuilding

the tip of his nose as best as possible. Rick went on to make a complete recovery and was eventually adopted into a forever home.

The story about Rick was picked up by the local media and a lot of attention was brought to the rescue group and rewards were even posted for information leading to the arrest of the individual responsible for his injuries. No arrests were ever made, despite quite a lot of media attention.

But it was a moment out of the spotlight which really tugged at our heartstrings. Having heard about Rick, Tony LaRussa made arrangements to meet him during his recovery. Tony had Rick brought to Busch Stadium one afternoon when there would be no cameras or reporters around to witness the meeting. All Tony did was take Rick to the lush outfield grass and play ball with him out of the spotlight.

This brief meeting in Busch Stadium was witnessed by only a few people, but that wasn't what was important. This man, with so much responsibility and notoriety, just wanted this poor dog to have fun and realize that not all humans were like the one who had harmed him. I already was of the opinion that Tony LaRussa was one of the greatest minds in baseball. Now, I was of the opinion that he had one of the biggest hearts.

IT DON'T MEAN A THING
IF YOU AIN'T GOT THE RING

There is no denying that St. Louis is a sports town. We fans have a love affair with our hometown Cardinals, and Blues. Well, we also loved our Rams, but thank you Stan Kroenke for moving them away. But St. Louis will always be first and foremost a baseball town. It has been said by professional athletes, sports writers, broadcasters, and even fans of other teams, that our city has some of the best and most knowledgeable fans in baseball. And the Cardinals have rewarded those great fans with a number of world championships, second only to the New York Yankees. Over the years, I've had the privilege of meeting several professional athletes and coaches, while taking care of their pets, including fan favorites Jack "The Ripper" Clark, and Rick Ankiel.

Another notable person who came into the clinic was Dave Duncan, the legendary pitching coach for the Cardinals. After joining the Cardinals, while also thinking ahead to his retirement, Mr. Duncan and his wife resided in Southwest Missouri on Table Rock Lake. During the baseball season Mr. Duncan spent his summers in a luxury St. Louis apartment. After moving down to Kimberling City on Table Rock Lake, they became good friends with Ross, one of my best friends and a classmate from veterinary school. For some time, Mr. Duncan and his wife had been taking their two Labradoodles to see Ross at Kimberling Animal Clinic. One of the Duncan's dogs had a condition called Megaesophagus, which caused it to regurgitate food if it ate too quickly. The dog needed to be fed in an upright position and closely monitored for aspiration pneumonia. Mrs. Duncan and the dogs would occasionally come to St. Louis during the baseball season, and during those times Ross arranged for me to assist them with their veterinary care and boarding.

Because of the special needs of one of their dogs, the Duncans came by to meet our staff and tour the clinic, prior to the dogs boarding. Dave and his wife were very nice and seemed quite comfortable with us. We gave them a tour of the clinic and discussed the care their dogs

174

would require, assuring them that we had experience dealing with megaesophagus. During the visit, we all couldn't help but notice that Dave was wearing his 2006 World Series Championship Ring. If you've ever seen a picture of such a ring you know that it is nearly impossible to miss. They're freakishly huge, adorned with gold and plenty of diamonds.

As they were about to leave, one of my staff got the nerve to ask Dave about his ring. He graciously took it off and allowed several of my staff members to try it on. The ring weighed a ton and it dwarfed their fingers, and it was amazing to see it up close. My mother, who was still working at the clinic, remarked to Dave that it must be really hard to wear. I responded, "No mom, it is really hard to get one of those rings, but really easy to wear one."

Vaccination clinic for Gateway Pet Guardians, working with Carrie Gravette,
one of the veterinary technicians from Hillside Animal Hospital

THE OBSCENE PHONE CALL

One evening, a client of ours named Rich arrived home from work just as the evening news was coming on. He remembered that a segment involving our clinic, Hillside Animal Hospital, and Randy Grim, the founder of Stray Rescue of St. Louis, was due to be featured on the six o'clock news that evening. Rich picked up his phone to call Mary Ellen Grim, Randy's mother and also a client of ours, to make sure she knew it was going to be televised and would be watching. Just as Mary Ellen's answering machine clicked on, Rich noticed the news segment involving us had begun. It was a story about the stray dog situation in our area and Randy was being interviewed by a local reporter. Soon after Randy, I too was interviewed about a unique medical problem affecting the stray dogs in the area. Rich decided to hold the phone up to the TV speakers so Mary Ellen, who clearly wasn't home, could at least hear her son and me on the news.

Several days later, we all happened to be together at a small fund-raising party for Stray Rescue and Rich suddenly remembered Mary Ellen had never returned his call. He asked if she'd received his phone message from the other evening. She replied that she hadn't received any messages from him. Confused, Rich asked again if she was positive she hadn't received any messages that evening. Mary Ellen was positive that she had not received any phone messages from Rich in the last several days. After some deliberation, she recalled a message on her answering machine that she described it as being so obscene she decided to quickly erase it. She was rather embarrassed and upset to have received such an indecent phone call. Rich was very confused and he tried to explain what he had done when he called and had to leave a message. Rich was puzzled that Mary Ellen didn't recognize our voices over the answering machine, and I was doubly confused because I didn't have a clue as to what they both were talking about. I was intrigued though about the crude message that had made its way onto Mary Ellen's answering machine.

It wasn't until a few minutes later that I put two and two together. I remembered that my interview on the evening news concerned TVT, or Transmissible Venereal Tumor, a very rare and unusual type of cancer that is sexually transmitted between dogs. It is a condition common in the Third World and Caribbean but definitely not in the St. Louis region. For some reason, which is still unexplained, Stray Rescue and particularly Hillside were dealing with a very large number of cases of this very rare condition in the stray dog population. I could just picture Mary Ellen coming home, seeing the message light blinking on her machine, getting excited about some friend calling her, pressing the message button, and hearing about "tumors growing on penises and vulvas, being transmitted sexually due to unprotected sex." I think I would have erased it too.

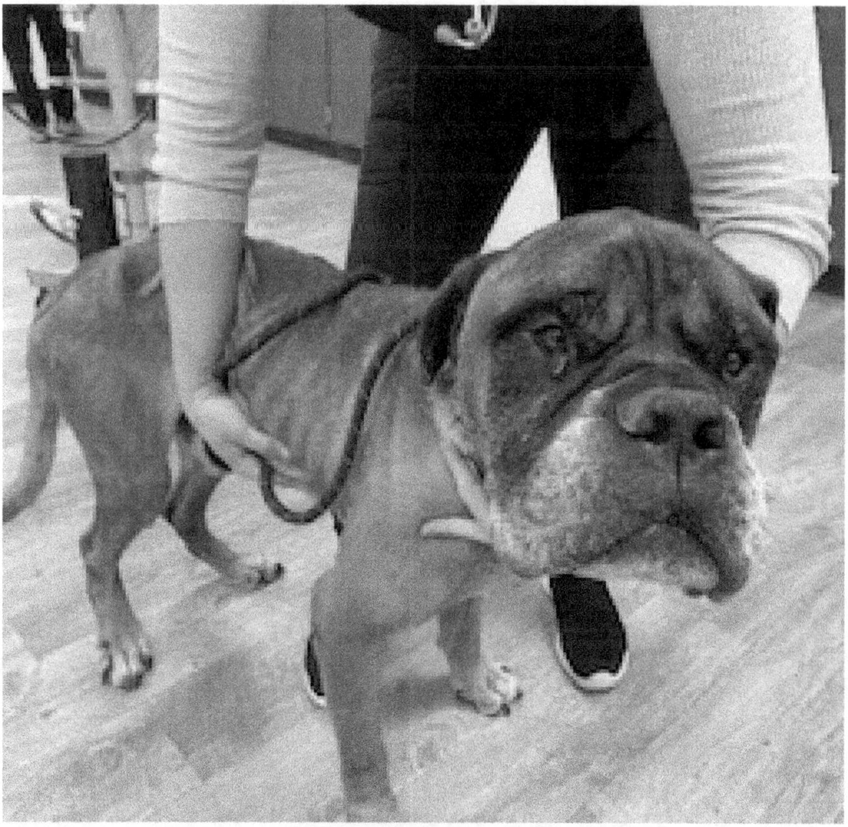

NO PRESSURE WHATSOEVER

I have worked a lot in the past with Randy Grim, the founder of Stray Rescue of St. Louis. Randy can be a bit of a polarizing figure in the veterinary community, but I have no doubt whatsoever about the size of his heart. He has done some tremendous work in the animal welfare community and the legacy of that good work will always be remembered. One of my favorite stories concerning Randy is about Quentin, the miracle dog. One day Randy received a phone call from the city pound supervisor. The strangest thing had just occurred and the supervisor wanted Randy to come over right away.

When Randy arrived at the pound the supervisor explained why Randy had been called over. Seven dogs had been scheduled for euthanasia that morning. They had been at the city pound for a certain amount of time and unfortunately, had not been adopted. Therefore, it was now time for them to be humanely euthanized. A city pound employee sedated the dogs and loaded them into the gas chamber. I know that sounds gruesome, but carbon monoxide was considered an acceptable form of euthanasia at the time. I'm happy to report that soon after this story broke, the city of St. Louis abolished the gas chamber. This would have never been achieved without the efforts of Randy and Quentin.

The seven dogs were loaded in, the gas chamber was started, and the employee went about her business for the 20 or 30 minutes it took to run its cycle. When she came back and opened the door, to her disbelief there was one dog sitting up in the back, wagging its tail at the worker, among the other six dead dogs in the chamber.

I cannot imagine the shock upon opening the door and finding out a dog survived the gas chamber. There were all kinds of theories put forth about how he could have survived, considering the other dogs died. I have since heard of this kind of thing happening elsewhere but no one

can offer an explanation. Nonetheless, that's when the supervisor called Randy. He had already been very active in the community and helped facilitate the rescue and adoption of many animals from the pound before they reached the end of the line. The city pound was not about to subject this miracle dog to the gas chamber again. This dog survived for a reason. Randy came over and immediately fell in love with the miracle dog and its will to live.

Randy immediately brought the dog to the clinic so we could check him out. He was in great shape and we genuinely couldn't find anything wrong, nor any obvious clues as to how he had survived. I suppose it's one of those unexplainable medical miracles. The dog was named Quentin, because Randy figured he had escaped death, just as if he had escaped prison. San Quentin is a notoriously large and tough prison in the state of California.

The story of Quentin reached a national level. He was even featured in *People* magazine and was flown around the country for interviews, so to speak, with his new owner Randy. He actually began to be called Quentin, the Miracle Dog. Quentin eventually signed a contract to be the spokesdog for a group known as In Defense of Animals. He continued to be in demand for appearances nationwide. When he traveled around the country, and even internationally, he had a seat of his own right next to Randy in first class.

For a long time Randy continued to bring Quentin into the clinic for us to take care of him. The crux of this story concerns the day it finally came time for Quentin to be neutered. Now, we have a good clinic and practice high-quality medicine, but the stress level at the clinic was a little high the day of Quentin's surgery. I told my team to bring their A game. I wanted to avoid being in the national headlines.

I could just see it now. "Dog who survives gas chamber dies under anesthesia at Dr. Ed's." Now, that is pressure.

IT'S RAINING PUPPIES

I first met David and Kelly Backes, who later became my best clients, when we were all on the board of directors for Five Acres Animal Shelter. It was one of several shelters I volunteered for, and was asked to serve on the board of directors. Not only did I gain two new friends, I was also able to meet Mark Buerhle, a major league baseball player whose wife was also on the board. One night Kelly invited the board members and spouses to the hockey game, and we sat in a luxury box with all the food and drink we wanted. I drank beer and ate chicken wings with Mark Buerhle and cheered on the St. Louis Blues. I know, it is not the biggest thrill for the average person, but for a big sports fan like me, it was a double dose of fun. This guy has pitched a couple of no-hitters and could possibly end up in the Hall of Fame. And I drank Budweiser with him.

At the time Kelly was attending nursing school and doing a clinical rotation in East St. Louis, IL. This is right across the Mississippi River from St. Louis, and is widely known as an economically distressed area. It is the main the service area now of Gateway Pet Guardians, the organization I ended up working for after selling my practice. Due to the stray dog problem which plagued that area at the time, good-hearted Kelly rescued an obviously pregnant stray dog she had befriended while driving home from work one day.

The stray dog that Kelly picked up and took into their nice home decided that it was a good place and time to go into labor just a few days later. Kelly called me late at night and I met her and David at the clinic. After determining quickly that the dog would need a C-section to successfully deliver the pups, I contacted two of my technicians, a married couple named Matt and Melissa, who lived close by, and graciously agreed to come in to help with the surgery.

We successfully delivered 12 pups that night by C-section. It was quite a sight, with me pulling pup after pup after pup out of the extremely enlarged uterus and handing them off to my techs, David, and Kelly. Everyone had their hands full reviving pups with warm towels. To see this big, strong, professional athlete getting very excited as he witnessed

the miracle of birth was a lot of fun. He even took videos of the action on his cell phone, and joined in with the resuscitation efforts. Kelly, the nursing student, was a great help and was just as excited as her husband. Of course, they ended up taking the mom and all 12 pups back to their big house and fostering them. This mother dog had really moved up in the world, off of the streets into a nice neighborhood and a warm home.

A couple of nights later, I was watching the Blues game on TV. During one of the intermissions between periods, the announcers were interviewing David, who gave a big shout out to Hillside Animal Hospital for what we had done a few days earlier. He even showed a couple of clips from the videos he took of all the pups after the surgery. I know we all do what we do because we love animals and do not necessarily expect thanks, but it was very cool to be recognized, especially on TV by someone famous.

Another story with David and Kelly involved puppies and a fostered dog, a beagle mix named Marty. The dog had been into the clinic and was tested for heartworms, dewormed, and vaccinated and was thought to be healthy. Unbeknownst to all of us, she was pregnant at the time of rescue. A couple of weeks later, Marty suddenly went into labor and delivered several stillborn pups. Kelly, being a nurse with a big heart, immediately picked up the pups, and tried to do mouth to mouth resuscitation, unfortunately to no avail. It turned out that Marty had a disease called brucellosis.

Brucellosis is a bacterial infection that is spread through sexual behavior and infects, among other areas of the body, the genital tract. It is fairly common in the stray dog population we deal with. In pregnant dogs it usually causes stillbirths and abortions, in male dogs it causes infection of the testicles, and it both sexes it can cause infections of the vertebral spine. The species of brucellosis that affects dogs is potentially transmissible to people and can be a serious issue. We take the possibility that a disease is zoonotic very seriously. The greatest concentration of the bacteria would be unfortunately in the deceased pups and the afterbirth.

Kelly and David brought the mom and the dead puppies to the clinic. After making sure the mother dog was okay and getting her situated, I had to switch modes from being a guardian of animal health to becoming a guardian of public health as it says in our veterinary oath. I proceeded to have a discussion with them about brucellosis and its potential for human infection. We immediately took blood samples from the dog and sent them off to the lab. I advised the clients to talk to their doctors and report the potential exposure.

Kelly, having the greatest risk of exposure, was immediately tested and put on a very long course of prophylactic antibiotics. She never tested positive for the disease, thank goodness. David, who had limited exposure, was also put on antibiotics as was the rookie hockey player who happened to be living in their house at the time, but probably never left the couch or his video games to see what all the fuss was about. Did I mention that David had just signed a multi-year, multimillion-dollar contract and been elected as team captain? Do you think the team was concerned about protecting their investment?

I take zoonotic diseases (diseases which can be spread from animals to people), very seriously in my practice. We worked with clients living with HIV and AIDS whose immune systems may be compromised, so we did everything to ensure their pets, which may be their only support group, maintained optimal health for their mutual benefit, therefore preserving the human/animal bond. I have personally treated numerous dogs with brucellosis and have never gotten sick. Although it is theoretically possible for the species that affects dogs to affect humans, it has never been proven outside of a laboratory setting.

The moral of the story was that everyone remained healthy. Marty was just fine, and ended up being treated, spayed, and eventually adopted by David and Kelly. She enjoyed a long happy life living it up and being pampered. The clinic instituted a new policy after this incident to test every pregnant stray for brucellosis prior to the dog going into a foster home. Of course, most ended up being spayed eventually, which reduces the possibility of spread, but we did not want to take any

more chances with regard to human health. We called our new policy the Backes Brucellosis Rule.

There is an unwritten rule in hockey that all injuries that players get are never fully disclosed to the media and especially to the other team. This is especially true during the playoffs. Any injury report released to the media, usually references the ubiquitous "upper body injury." I kept scanning the papers for several weeks after that incident looking for my client's name, but thankfully he remained healthy and in the lineup. I did not want to be the cause of the home team losing one of its best and favorite players due to a dog venereal disease. But I would have chuckled a little bit if it had been reported as a lower body injury.

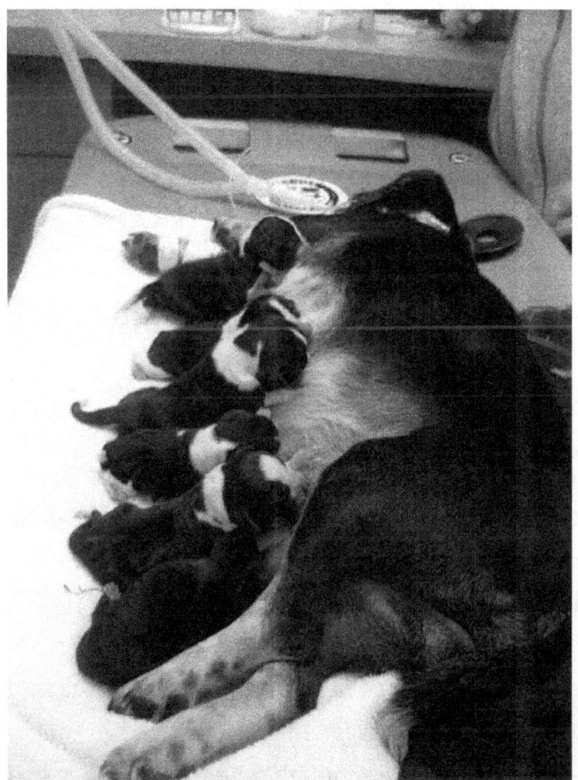

Mother beagle and pups recovering from a successful C-section

THE BEST SEAT IN THE HOUSE, ER, CAR

This story is about a good person trying to do a good thing, with a not so good result. I've mentioned a couple of our best clients, David and Kelly, in a previous story. David was captain of the St. Louis Blues. Kelly, his wife, is considered the "First Lady" of the team. Both of them graciously give with both their time and money and are exceptionally active in the local animal welfare community. There is a saying that goes, "Good things happen to good people," but another saying I like to remember is, "No good deed goes unpunished." The animal in this story doesn't have a happy ending, but it wasn't due to a lack of altruistic effort. I'm not here to make light of the fact that an animal died, but rather to illustrate the lengths certain people will go to help an animal in need.

One night Kelly was driving home with a friend when they witnessed a cat being struck by a car. The car didn't stop, but in all fairness the passengers might not have realized they'd even hit a cat. It's also possible they didn't care and chose to keep driving. Kelly immediately stopped and went to the aid of the cat. Right away, it was clear that the cat was dying from serious head injuries. Kelly gently picked up the cat, wrapped it in whatever she had in her trunk, and laid it on the front seat of her brand-new Mercedes SUV.

At this point, she called and asked if I would meet her at the clinic. As Kelly was telling me about the cat, it ended up expiring. Kelly still wanted to go to the clinic to see if the cat had a microchip. Even though she couldn't save the cat, she thought that perhaps she could bring some closure to a family who was dearly missing it. I was in a meeting, but told Kelly I would meet her at the clinic in a short while.

Kelly and her friend decided to stop at Kelly's house to check on her own pets before coming to the clinic. They left the cat in the car, wrapped up, on the front passenger seat. Even though they were only gone for a few minutes, it was enough time for them to learn an important lesson in physiology. When an animal expires, whether through natural causes, euthanasia, or a tragic accident such as this, it is not unusual for the animal to release urine from the bladder. Kelly returned to the

cat to find that urine had soaked all the way through the cat's wrappings, the seat of the car, and all over the floor mats. The passenger seat of this Mercedes SUV model is heated, cooled, fully adjustable, and made of expensive leather. Heck, I bet the floor mats are made of leather too. Corinthian leather, for all I know.

When I made it to the clinic, Kelly and her friend were parked and in the midst of a massive clean-up project. I tried to help them by gathering several kinds of enzymatic cleansers that the clinic uses for when cats urinate outside of their litter box. But this was way out of the box. I forgot to mention, the cat involved turned out to be an intact tomcat. Anyone who works with cats knows what tomcat urine smells like. Once at a veterinary conference in Las Vegas I went to the hotel where Siegfried and Roy were playing. Their white tigers were on display in the lobby behind thick plexiglass partitions from floor to ceiling. As I walked by one of the tigers backed up to the partition and sprayed urine to mark his territory. Boy, was I glad the partitions were not only unbreakable, but smell proof. Anyway, despite our best efforts, there'd be no getting that pungent smell out of Kelly's seat. Kelly was left with no choice but to confess to David what had happened. David, knowing all about his wife and her big heart, was very understanding.

The car was eventually taken back to the Mercedes dealership. Would you believe that a new seat for a Mercedes SUV has to be ordered and shipped from Germany? Can you see the dollars adding up? The new seat cost them several thousand dollars. All this happened because Kelly was trying to be a good Samaritan. She said despite the outcome, she'd do it all over again, but this time she'd keep a cat carrier in her car.

I'm good friends with Kelly and David, so I've ridden in her car on several occasions. I have to be honest though, since this incident occurred, I haven't been back in that passenger seat. Next time we go somewhere together, I won't be so quick to yell, "Shotgun" for the front seat. At least, until I feel it first. Or smell it.

THE APPENDIX CAN WAIT

One weekend I happened to be out of town attending my veterinary school reunion, when David called. When your best client calls, you take the call. Of course, you then show all of your friends who just called you. Yes, it's the ultimate name-dropping, but it never fails to impress.

David was calling to let me know that he was at the hospital with Kelly, who'd gotten sick and needed emergency surgery to have her appendix removed. I asked if they needed any help with their animals, because it was the least I could do. I was only a couple of hours away and was getting ready to come home when he called.

David and Kelly did need help with an animal, just not one of their own. Kelly, who was on her way to the operating room, had struck up a conversation with one of her nurses. The nurse proceeded to tell Kelly about one of her dogs who had an injured eye, yet the nurse did not have enough money to get it taken care of. Kelly instructed David to call me and ask if I'd see the dog and take care of it at their expense. She would not let them take her to surgery until she knew that the nurse's dog would be taken care of.

I got the information from David to contact the nurse, and I assured him that I would call and see her dog that afternoon. I guess that was all Kelly needed to hear, because she promptly went to surgery and had her appendix removed. She made a full recovery and was back to rescuing animals after only a few weeks.

We made it back home, and saw the nurse and her dog at the clinic as promised. Her dog had been bitten by another dog around one of its eyes over a week before. The eye had gotten infected and by the time I saw the dog, it was too late to save the dog's eye. We treated the infection with antibiotics, and I explained to the nurse that we'd have to surgically remove the dog's eye the next day to save him from serious pain and suffering. The eye surgery was successful, and the dog went home that day, making a full recovery from its injury.

This story illustrates the depth of some people's love for animals. Kelly put the needs of an injured dog over her own needs. As much as I love animals, I think that if my appendix was in danger of bursting, I would not be thinking about my dog at home. I'd be begging the doctor to get in there and take it out, after begging them to give me something for the pain.

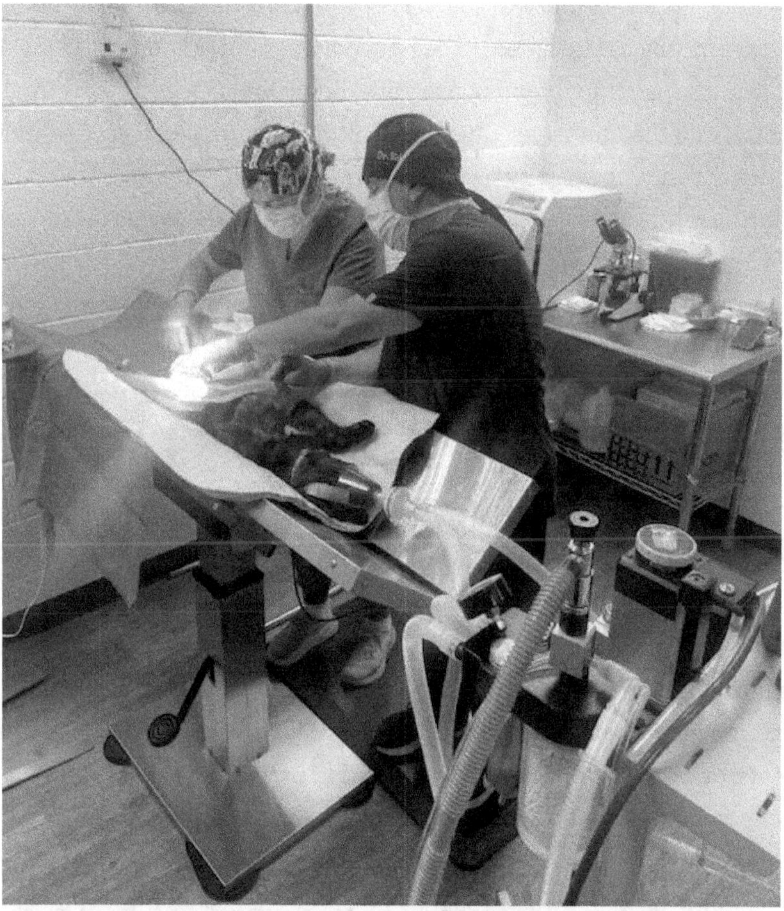

Nina performing one of her first surgeries(with some help from dad)

HIP CZECH

Recently St. Louis lost a beloved sports icon when Bob Plager, one of the original St. Louis Blues hockey players, passed away. Bob had retired in 1978, but so loved St. Louis that he decided to stay here. The city paid him back handsomely with all the love and admiration afforded to sports heroes, and he has remained a fan favorite. Every hockey fan in St. Louis has a Bob Plager memory to share. He was one of the last hockey players, specifically defensemen, to use a hip check as a way of thwarting an opponent's rush into the offensive zone. Some unsuspecting forward, rushing into the offensive end of the rink with their head down, would suddenly be flying head over heels as Bob perfectly laid him out with a well-timed hip check. All legal of course, but the practice has fallen out of favor in recent years.

Bob embodied what old time hockey was all about, as evidenced one night when the Blues were playing in Philadelphia, known to have some rowdy fans if you know what I mean. Something happened on the ice to set off the fans, and they responded by bombarding the Blues bench area with anything handy, including beer bottles. One of the bottles struck the Blues' coach, and the players—led by Bob Plager and Noel Picard—climbed into the stands to go after the offending fans. There were the Blues, in their uniforms and skates, climbing over the plexiglass and chasing the fans in the stands who had thrown the bottles. After the game, the Philadelphia police actually came into the locker room and carted several of the Blues to the station, still in their uniforms. Reminds me of one of my favorite movies, *Slap Shot*. Old time hockey, yeah!

I once sat next to Bob at a charity event and I was like a little kid again, meeting one of my idols. I am not big on autographs, but for me just shaking his hand was enough. One of my clients at Hillside, Barrett Jackman, former Blues defenseman, told me a great story about Bob. Barrett ended up wearing the same number 5 on his jersey as Bob did during his career. When it came time to retire Bob's number, Barrett had the pleasure of being the one to tell Bob the news. It was a heartwarming moment for the whole city as Bob was loved that much.

Headquartered in St. Louis, Nestle Purina has a long and productive relationship with Hillside Animal Hospital. At one time in their history the company was the owner of the Blues team and helped keep the team in St. Louis, when there was chance that the team was going to be lost to another city. They are one of the biggest pet food companies in the world, I strongly believe they are the best pet food manufacturer, but that is not to take away from several others which are also very good. I guess I am just a hometown kind of guy. Nestle Purina used to bring over visiting veterinarians and other dignitaries from all over the world to Hillside for a tour of a "typical" animal hospital and we were proud to oblige them. On numerous occasions veterinarians were brought over for a tour and a question-and-answer period with us at Hillside. Even the CEO and many of the top "suits" in the company have paid us visits in the past. It afforded the vets and executives a chance to meet colleagues from other parts of the world and exchange practice and business ideas. We at Hillside were always very proud that Nestle thought so highly of us.

One such visit included a group of fifteen vets from Czechoslovakia. Several, but not all of the group, spoke English, so we were able to communicate, with those group members serving as translators. I have come to find out that most veterinarians around the world are the same as we deal with common issues on a daily basis. I seemed to hit it off remarkably well with this group, as they were easy-going and gregarious. They informed me that the group was going to the St. Louis Blues hockey game that night and invited me to attend. I just happened to have tickets to the game already and told them that I would meet up with them at the game. Then, after the visit I called my good friend, Kelly Backes, wife of David, the team captain, to arrange a special surprise for the Czech vets after the game.

A good time was had by all as the Blues won the game against our big rivals, the Chicago Blackhawks, 4-2. When the game was over, I informed the Czech contingent that we were invited down to the locker room to meet the players. On the way down, the head of security for the Blues (also a client of mine) arranged a photo opportunity on the players' bench.

Once at the locker room the vets got
to meet with David Backes of course,
but then an even more special surprise
occurred. Two of the Blues players, goalie
Jaroslav Halak and defenseman Roman
Polak, who are both from Czechoslovakia, came to the meet the vets. All were
thrilled to be able to meet these players,
and both sides were thrilled to be able to
converse in their native language so far
from home. I had no idea what was being
said, not that it mattered in the least. The
smiles on everyone's faces said it all.

The night could not have been any
better, even if it had been written as
a Hollywood script. I almost forgot to
mention that the two stars of the game
that night, chosen by the sports press,
were none other than Jaroslav Halak and
Roman Polak. A couple of months later I
received a package from Czechoslovakia
in the mail. Inside was a picture from that
night with the Czech vet team and me at
the hockey game, all crammed into the
elevator taking us down the locker room.
Everyone in the photo is wearing a huge
smile after a great victory, including the
St. Louis Blues employee running the
elevator. It is a cherished memento of a
great night. It has been said that sports
transcend language barriers. Maybe veterinary medicine does too. Or at least the
combination of the two does.

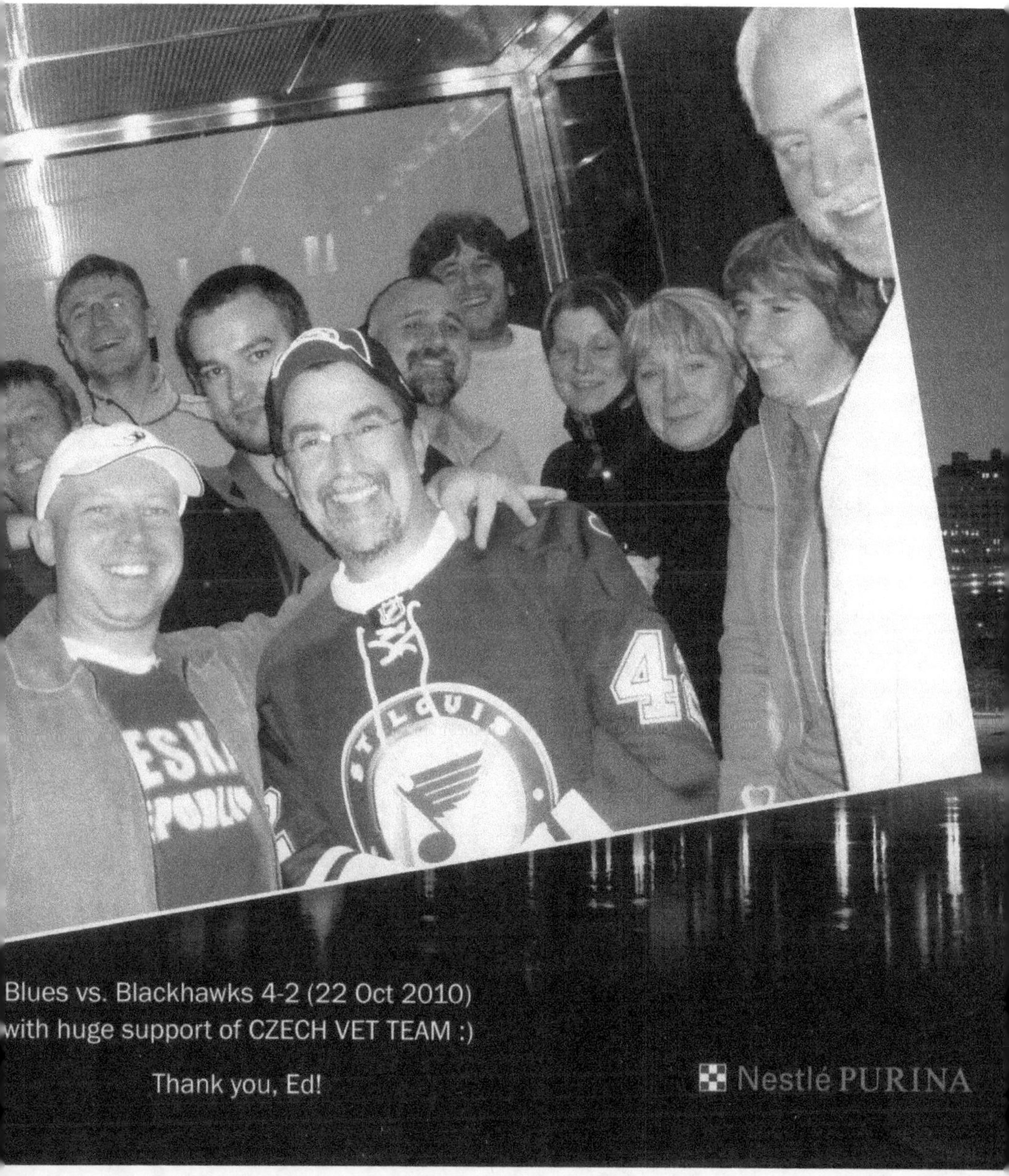

Blues vs. Blackhawks 4-2 (22 Oct 2010)
with huge support of CZECH VET TEAM :)
Thank you, Ed!
Nestlé PURINA

RESCUE ME

POUR SOME SUGAR ON ME

Music is an important part of my life, but that being said, I have absolutely no musical talent. I like to say that I can play a mean radio. I can sing with the best of them, but only alone, in my car. I am the type of person who would much rather be listening to '80s on 8, or KSHE-95, Classic Rock Radio, then talk radio any day of the week. A couple of years ago, I had the great fortune to take a pilgrimage to the Rock & Roll Hall of Fame. I spent almost 5 hours there, visiting every single exhibit and watching every video I could. It really was a "religious experience" for me.

I always have music on when I am doing surgery, and will commonly play Name That Tune with whichever technician is stuck with me that day. After a few times, they start to recognize the songs and the game gets old. But the music gets me motivated and keeps me going during long surgery days. Techs say they know who is doing surgery without even looking by listening to what music is playing.

One day I got a call from Janet, the Outreach Coordinator of Gateway Pet Guardians, who dealt with the public in our service area, handling phone calls about pet emergencies and other issues. Whenever my phone rang and I saw that Janet was calling, I knew instinctively that my day just got more interesting. She proceeded to tell me about a young puppy with "its thing hanging out," and I knew immediately she was talking about a condition known as paraphimosis. This is a situation where a male dog gets an erection of his penis, and then the penis gets stuck outside of the prepuce and cannot return to normal size. It is obviously uncomfortable for the dog and if left for too long, can be serious. I told her I was not busy and could meet her at the clinic in a few minutes. I hopped in my car, turned on the radio, and started singing along to the Archies' "Sugar, Sugar."

The dog Janet brought into the clinic did indeed have paraphimosis, but the fact that it was a young puppy was an unusual presentation for

this condition. With some sedation and manipulation of the tissues the penis can generally be returned to its normal position and everyone is happy. There were some giggles among the volunteers when I explained what the condition was and how I was going to fix it.

Unfortunately, this was a difficult case and the usual manipulations were not working. I looked for other contributing causes, such as something like hair strands wrapped around the penis, and could find no obvious reason why I could not return the penis into the prepuce. I worked diligently for what seemed like a long time and started to consider the possibility that I may need to resort to surgery to enlarge the prepuce opening to get the job done.

I once again channeled the spirit of James Herriot and remembered one of his stories. When faced with a very large, swollen organ that had prolapsed out of the body, he turned to an old trick to shrink it in size and make the job easier. So, I went to the break room, got some sugar, and covered the swollen and edematous penis with it. The sugar acts through osmosis to remove some of the tissue fluid from the swollen organ and helps return it to normal size. Knowing the physiology of what causes an erection to occur, some of my veterinary friends are shaking their heads at my MacGyvering. But I thought what the heck, we should give it a try.

I finally was able to return the penis to its normal position in the prepuce and then applied a very loose suture to close the opening slightly to help keep it in place for a few days. Of course, my sugar trick brought out more laughter and giggles from the crowd which seemed to have formed around me. And then the crude and inappropriate comments started. I had tried my best to ignore the silliness and concentrated on the job at hand. That is until I finished and heard what was playing on the radio in the background. When I brought it to the attention of the crowd, all hell broke loose, all bets were off on the social correctness of the situation. The song was "Pour Some Sugar on Me," by Def Leppard. Sweet!!!

JOHN JACOB DINGLEBERRY SCHMIDT

Maybe you remember singing the song as a child, "John Jacob Jingle-heimer Schmidt," about a little boy who shares a common name with the title character and is recognized because of that shared name. For some reason this song always came to mind whenever I encountered a dingle-berry in practice. I am sure those of you of the veterinary persuasion know what I am talking about, but for those uninformed individuals, a dingleberry is a piece of feces that is stuck on the hair around the anus. It is not fun for the animal, or the person designated to clean the area, but it is an easy diagnosis and easy fix.

I had seen several cases when an owner believes that a mass near the rear end of their beloved pet is cancer. Being able to remove the mass during the examination using only electric clippers, is very satisfactory and rewarding, but perhaps a little embarrassing for the owner. Most of the time this occurs in a longer-haired dog or cat who is a little over-weight and is unable to do any personal grooming. I always enjoy joking around with the clients when I am finished doing such a simple job and they will ask how much they owe me. I like to respond, "Well, this ex-tensive surgery to remove this dangerous mass from the rear end of your pet will only cost (insert here some ridiculously large sum of money)." Obviously, they know I am joking and are relieved that it was not as seri-ous as they thought. I like to say that one of the most important things I dispense is peace of mind.

Occasionally, the presenting complaint about a pet is constipation. The pet may actually have diarrhea, causing inflammation, irritation and spasms which can appear as strain from constipation. So, the first step is to determine if the pet is really constipated or has colitis. Sometimes the pet will actually have a fecal impaction around the rear end, preventing it from defecating, such as this story.

All of which leads to a case encountered one day while on commu-nity outreach for Gateway Pet Guardians with my good friend Janet. It

occurred the summer I was recovering from rotator cuff surgery, and my right arm was in a sling, to remind me to avoid sudden movements in the wrong direction while the shoulder was healing. Janet had received a call from a community member about a dog trying to defecate, but nothing was coming out. We went to assess the situation and to determine if the dog needed a full-service veterinary visit. It was a warm summer day and I was enjoying my time with Janet, riding around in her cluttered car, hitting every pot hole possible, and jarring my surgically repaired shoulder. We went to the assigned address and found the client and patient, an older Shi Tzu, probably as wide as she was long, waiting on the porch. I like to say she would have made a good ottoman.

The dog seemed happy enough, but the problem soon became evident. Around her anus was one of the largest fecal impactions I have ever encountered. It encompassed the entire rear end, from under the tail, down ventrally to her vulva bordering on both sides for several inches. The dog was in great need of grooming, as is common with patients in our service area, because unfortunately, these services were not readily available. I am very proud to say that Gateway Pet Guardians now offers grooming to our clients, and it has been well received.

After Janet and I assessed the situation I quickly determined that we did not have a pair of electric clippers, nor even have a pair of good scissors with us. A clipper is always preferable over a pair of scissors whenever attempting to remove a mat or a fecal impaction from an animal, as it is very easy to cut the skin with scissors and cause more damage. The owner provided us with some small safety scissors, the ones with blunted ends that school age children learn how to cut with. While Janet held the dog, I went to work, with those small scissors, carefully trimming the hair between the impacted feces and the skin. It was painstaking work that took over 45 minutes, as I was basically one-handed. And the fecal material that had caused the impaction was very soft. By the time we were finished, both Janet and I were very dirty and smelly. But the dog was happy, and immediately went out in the yard and did her business.

She needed some more grooming but was happy to be able to poop nonetheless.

When we were finished, I told Janet that we had to go back to the shelter and clean up before we could go to our usual lunch spot. There was no way I was going to Taco Bell looking and smelling like I did. I could just imagine the stares. But I got a smile out of Janet and the owner when I said that, "All is well when the end is well."

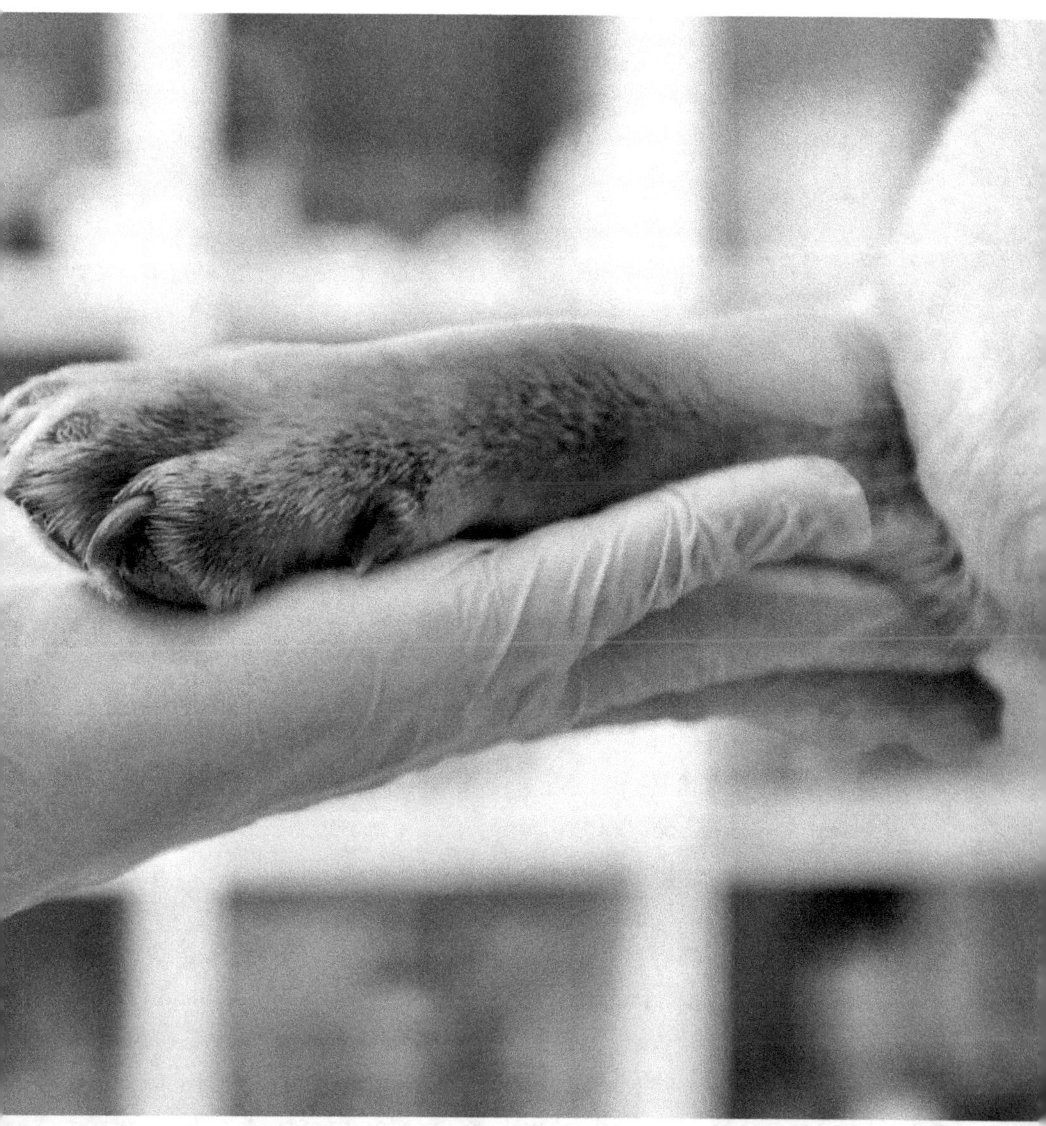

RESCUE ME

GIMME SHELTER

I have been a part of Gateway Pet Guardians since its incorporation in 2004. Gateway was formed to help support the rescue efforts of a wonderful woman named Peggy Hightower. Peggy took it upon herself to feed and rescue stray dogs in East St. Louis, Illinois. In that city, at the time, there was a serious stray dog problem, with packs of strays inhabiting the many vacant lots and abandoned houses there. Peggy went over to the "East Side," as it is known, on a daily basis, bringing food to numerous packs she would encounter, reportedly without missing a single day in over 2 years of visiting "her dogs." She would also rescue any sick or injured dogs and seek out veterinary care for them as needed.

Hillside Animal Hospital was the main clinic that offered discounted, if not free, veterinary care for the rescued dogs. I had worked with Peggy from the beginning, when her rescue efforts were being supported by Stray Rescue of St. Louis. Their main service area really was the City of St. Louis, and Peggy's work in East St. Louis took on its own identity that became supported by Gateway Pet Guardians. Other clinics also were used, but Hillside was the main provider of veterinary care. Our involvement with Gateway evolved over the years, and as the organization grew, I was eventually asked to be on the Board of Directors. I became a full-time employee of Gateway Pet Guardians in 2019 after selling my practice to my daughter.

Gateway was able to purchase a shuttered public grade school from the East St. Louis Board of Education and moved their base of operations in 2019. After a year of rehab/remodel we opened as the largest pet resource center, and the first veterinary clinic ever in the city. Currently, it is considered a low-cost wellness clinic, but more services and surgeries are being added all the time, and we still work with Hillside and other veterinary clinics if care is needed that we cannot provide. Gateway Pet Guardians also has a store with low-cost, but good quality, pet food available for purchase, as well as a pet food pantry for those owners who need the help due to financial concerns. And I am very proud to say

that we have a full-time social worker on staff to help with any needs or concerns of the pet owners that may arise.

The City of East St. Louis has welcomed us with open arms. Everyone from the pet owners and the politicians to the police and fire department are grateful for our presence in the community. In the early days, Gateway volunteers were known as the "dog people," or the ones who fed the strays and rescued the injured ones. Our focus area was East St. Louis, but the organization was actually based across the river in St. Louis, MO. Now with our physical location we are actively working where we need to be, and we have rapidly become a fixture in the community and really feel welcomed.

Our efforts over the years had gone a long way in controlling the stray dog problem in the area. The occasional stray will still be found, but due to our microchipping efforts, will often turn out to be someone's pet who has escaped or gotten lost. But the decrease in the stray dog population has led to an increase in the stray cat population. We started a TNR (Trap, Neuter, and Release) program several years ago to deal with that issue and it continues today.

Multiple feral cat colonies are all over the city and most are managed by "caretakers" who feed and look after the cats in their colony. Gateway works with these caretakers by trapping, spaying and neutering the cats, and then returning the cats to where they live–thereby decreasing the number of litters. Colonies become more stable without a constant influx of new cats. Albeit a slightly controversial method of dealing with the stray cat overpopulation problem, it is the best that we can do for now.

Working with one such caretaker, volunteers from Gateway trapped a number of cats from a certain colony and transported them back to the shelter. Surgeries were done on all of them, their left ear was tipped to identify them as being altered, vaccinations were administered, and microchips were implanted to further identify where they originated. The day after their surgery the cats are all transported back to their colony and released onto familiar ground.

One cat that was being released darted from her trap as it was opened, but instead of running for cover in the yard she lived in prior to being trapped, she ran under the van. The volunteers could not see her there so they assumed she was in some bushes on the other side of the van. The rest of the cats were released without any issues, and the volunteers returned to the shelter and parked the van in its usual spot in our lot.

Two days later the alarm company notified us that an internal alarm had been tripped, indicating a possible intruder. Part of the property's security program includes inside and outside cameras set up at multiple locations. Employees could see that the "intruder" was actually a cat running around the hallways, triggering the motion detectors.

We accounted for all of the cats in their respective cages, then started a search. As our building encompasses over 50,000 square feet it is no small task to try and find a cat that doesn't want to be found. Every day we could find evidence that the cat had gotten into some food bag, or had left some solid or liquid evidence of being in the building. This went on for several days until we finally tried to set some live traps to try and catch our mystery guest.

We finally caught our "cat burglar" in one of the traps set in one of the areas we knew it frequented. To our surprise, the cat looked familiar and even had a tipped left ear. The cat was somewhat feral but allowed us to perform an examination and we found a microchip and evidence of a recent surgery. It turns out it was the same cat that ran under the van when it was being released back to its home.

Some of the employees viewed security videos from the time the van returned to the parking lot. A cat could be seen coming out from under the van and approaching the building. This solved part of the mystery, but not all. Somehow the cat must have crawled up under the van and hitched a ride back to the shelter. We have no idea how she did that without getting hurt, nor how the cat got into the building.

This cat must have decided that life in the shelter was not so bad, compared to a life on the streets. I mean, we did feed her a nice meal after her surgery, and the building does have working AC and furnaces. Maybe she somehow knew that life has to be better on the inside. The cat was given the name Martha. I can neither confirm nor deny the possibility that she was named after a certain television personality who may have spent some time locked up herself. Maybe she was just looking for her own Snoop Dog.

Me and my cat Helen

CONTRIBUTED STORIES FROM DR. MARK LUX AND DR. DALE DIESEL

Drs. Mark Lux and Dale Diesel are two of my best friends in the veterinary profession. They are part of the group I have mentioned in the book as getting together for lunch once a month. Once over lunch at a popular restaurant we were discussing the latest abscess that we had popped open and the color and the smell of the pus that came shooting out. It was then that we noticed a table of little old ladies sitting next to us asking the waiter if they could be moved to another table. Over the course of years, they have heard me talk of trying to write a book about the adventures we have all had in practice and I have decided to share some of their own stories included with my own. Despite the proximity of our practices, we became instant friends and remain friends to this day. I really want to thank them for helping me out as when I was first starting in practice and continuing to be my friend all these years. I am including a few of their stories because I just wanted to prove that my experiences were not unique but are probably happening across the country on a daily basis.

DR. MARK LUX

Do You Want Fries with That?

We had been working with a ferret rescue group (it is surprising the number of stray ferrets that are out there) for a few years. The group was organized by an individual and he put up his own money for the start-up costs. They were trying to raise money and asked if they could put a notice up on my bulletin board advertising a benefit barbecue in a few months. A client walked into the office and saw the notice for a ferret barbecue and with a straight face asked one staff member, "What does barbecued ferret taste like?"

When It Absolutely Has to Get There Overnight

Our office is next to a post office and a client was scheduled to bring their cat in for vaccinations. They decided to visit the post office first, so they took their crated cat into the post office with them. Standing in line at the Post Office (as we all have done), a customer asked the client what they were doing there. They responded that they were picking up a package. The customer responded, "I didn't know you could send animals through the mail!"

Oh What a Relief It Is

Years ago, there was a drug called "Cortaba" and it was used for the treatment of arthritis in dogs. It was a combination of aspirin and prednisone. A very effective drug but nowadays it is known that the use of those two drugs together greatly increases the risk of stomach ulceration. Back then an older gentleman came in to have his dog's Cortaba prescription refilled. I happened to be in the front office at the time and he said, "Doc, I accidentally took some of that arthritis medicine for Fido and I've never felt better." After that we kept a very close eye on how often he had the prescription refilled.

Life is Like a Box of Chocolates

Recently we removed a foreign body from a dog's stomach and small intestine. The dog is epileptic and is on anti-seizure medication. One of the side effects of this medication is a ravenous appetite, so needless to say this dog would eat pretty much anything. No foreign bodies showed up on an x-ray, but since the dog kept vomiting, we decided to do exploratory surgery. I removed a plastic chin strap from a football helmet. When I told the owner what it was, she said that they had put some of their son's football equipment in an empty chocolate box for storage. The dog got a hold of the box and I guess he thought he was munching on candy.

DR. DALE DIESEL

Tastes Like Corn!

My first 5 years out of practice was in a mixed animal practice and one of my responsibilities was performing surgeries on farm animals that were brought in to our clinic. One of the most common surgeries was correcting rectal prolapses on pigs. This condition was mostly seen in younger piglets, and occurred when pigs piled up on one another when the weather got cold. The poor pig on the bottom had so much pressure on his abdomen that something had to give and it was usually the rectum that prolapsed through the anus where it would then swell and not go back in. To be corrected surgically the pig was placed on a table with the head down, putting the anus and the prolapse in a position that the surgeon could work on it. One cold day in January, I was busy repairing one of these, when the pig held its breath and gave a mighty strain. Before I could move or block it, a stream of liquid pig manure hit me in the face, beard, and open mouth (sometimes you should just know when to keep your mouth shut). Being in the middle of the procedure, I couldn't just walk away. The farmer and my assistant just looked at me and there was a moment of silence as they watched me for my reaction. Spitting out what had entered my mouth, I just said "It tastes like corn", upon which they both doubled over in laughter. I don't recommend it but I can honestly say it doesn't taste as bad as it smells.

Hot On the Grill

Hogs raised in confinement many times were housed in building with slats to walk on and where they could comfortably support their weight and the urine and fecal material would drop into a pit below the floor. These pits were usually 6 to 8 feet deep and if they weren't pumped out often or if the ventilation in the building was poor, several different gases would accumulate, one of them being methane. One day, I was walking down the middle aisle of one of these buildings with the farmer discussing various health issues for his pigs. As the farmer finished his cigarette,

he stopped and taking careful aim, dropped it through one of the spaces between two slats. I happened to look down at that time and saw a wave of blue flame run the length of the building. Thankfully, the gas wasn't compressed which would have caused an explosion. But I did get an idea of what a hot dog must feel like on the grill.

CONTRIBUTED STORIES FROM DR. ROSS HENRY

One of my best friends from Veterinary School is Dr. Ross Henry. After practicing in St. Louis for a few years he bought a practice in Southwest Missouri in a town called Kimberling City on Table Rock Lake. He and his wife Pam have been enjoying life on the lake ever since and I remain good friends with them to this day. Ross and I talk all the time about the crazy things that can happen in practice and he has shared a couple of stories about his life as a practicing veterinarian. I have taken the liberty of writing down these stories as told to me by Ross. I hope you will enjoy them as much as I did.

Blue is My Favorite Color

Veterinarians love new toys. When I say new toys, I'm referring to the latest technology. We all love to acquire new instruments, monitoring devices, or tools to make our lives easier. But one can't help and show off a little bit when they get new toys. Like I always say, "He who has the most toys, wins." Ross had recently purchased a new electro-surgical unit. This machine uses an electrical current to simultaneously cut tissue and cauterize blood vessels. This means a veterinarian is able to perform a bloodless surgery, or minimize the amount of bleeding throughout surgery. The electro-surgical unit can also be utilized to cauterize blood vessels during conventional surgery. I mean that even if you are not using it as a scalpel to cut tissue, it can still be used to cauterize blood vessels that are bleeding during other surgeries.

A few days after adding the new gadget to the clinic's collection, an elderly woman came in with her toy poodle for its annual physical exam and vaccinations. Ross performed the annual exam and found the dog to be in good shape, with the exception of a few little sebaceous adenomas on the dog's skin. Sebaceous adenomas are little cauliflower-like warts dogs will acquire on their skin as they age. These growths usually don't cause any problems, but occasionally they will start to bleed if they're bumped or are accidentally clipped while a dog is being groomed.

Ross, being the good veterinarian that he is, seized upon the opportunity of explaining to the client just what the little growths were. He explained that since the dog visits the groomer regularly, it may be wise to remove them. He advised the elderly woman that the procedure could be completed in a designated exam room with her toy poodle fully awake, unable to feel a thing. The owner was quite impressed and agreed to follow through with the procedure.

The dog had a small amount of hair clipped away from 2 of the warts on his back. My friend had his new electro-surgical unit, all plugged in and ready to go. Ross scrubbed the dog's skin with some antimicrobial solution, and then doused it liberally with alcohol. Next, he injected some local anesthetic into the site to numb it up. Finally, he reached for his new toy.

Unfortunately, he didn't wait long enough for the alcohol to dry. As soon as the hot electrical surgical tip hit the dog, the alcohol burst into flames.

Now, don't be alarmed. It was on a very small section of the dog's skin, and it was immediately doused with a towel. The rest of the procedure went as planned with no more flammable mishaps.

The elderly client seemed nonetheless for wear, or blissfully unaware of the near tragedy. She was happy that her precious poodle was healthy and looked better than ever without those nasty warts.

Her only comment as she walked towards the door to leave, was how impressed she was with the doctor's newest instrument. It made such a pretty blue color when he worked on her dog.

Can You Hear Me Now?

A few years ago, my good friend and classmate Ross Henry attended a veterinary conference, and enrolled in a wet lab for veterinary dental procedures. A wet lab consists of learning about dental procedures during a lecture part, and then practicing the new techniques that you just learned about in a laboratory setting on specimens. It's hands-on-learning. The lectures and wet lab were taught by a nationally known veterinary dentist. Ross thoroughly enjoyed the entire experience and learned quite a lot. He was very excited to learn more about taking care of his patient's teeth, including new techniques for extracting teeth when necessary and caring for his patients' oral health. He seemed to get along well with the instructor, asking lots of good questions, even staying after lab to further discuss the class content.

The instructor appeared to also enjoy Ross's company, so they worked together for another hour and a half after the other attendees had left. It was quite stimulating having the opportunity to work with such an esteemed veterinarian. When they were finally finished, the veterinary dentist gave Ross his business card and told him to call any time and he'd be happy to assist him with any problems. Needless to say, Ross was quite thrilled, and left the wet lab with a renewed vigor to apply the new techniques learned that day.

A whole year went by before Ross had occasion to call the instructor. He happened to have a new case in for some dental work, and the dog had a particular orthodontic problem which would need fixing. Ross decided to call his new friend, the veterinary dentist, for some advice.

After searching on his desk, he finally found the business card. The dentist's office was in Colorado. It was now 10 AM in the Midwest, so he figured with it being 9 AM in Colorado, it wasn't too early to call. Every hard-working veterinarian, even one with a dental practice, had to be at work by 9.

Ross dialed the number and it rang, and rang, and rang. Finally, after about 12 rings, a seemingly groggy voice said, "Hello?"

The conversation went something like this from that point on.

"Is this Dr. Smith?"

"Yes, it is," the groggy voice answered.

"Dr. Smith, this is Dr. Ross Henry from Southwest Missouri. I met you last year at the Central Veterinary Conference, where I took part in your dental wet lab. You gave me your business card and told me I could call you at any time with dental questions. Do you remember me?"

"Yes, I guess I do," answered the groggy voice.

"Well, I have an interesting case here I would like to ask you about... so I called your office number. I thought since it was 9 AM in Colorado it was safe to call you."

"Well, the number on my business card is actually my cell phone number, but I am not in Colorado. I am in Honolulu, and it's 3 AM."

The rest of the conversation involved a lot of apologizing and embarrassment by Ross. Dr. Smith was most accommodating, but did ask Ross to call him back in about 6-7 hours when his brain would be more awake.

I can't honestly say if Ross ever called back Dr. Smith to ask his question. For all I know, he could have thrown out the business card, had plastic surgery to change his appearance, and changed his name in case he ever had the misfortune to run into the sleepy dentist again.

CONTRIBUTED STORY FROM DR. LARRY ZEIS

Dead Cat Anyone?

This particular story happened to another veterinary practitioner friend of mine named Dr. Larry Zeis. Larry was especially helpful to me when I first started practicing. Being a new graduate and a new business owner, there was obviously a lot I did not know, and a lot I did not know that I did not know, if you know what I mean. He was always there with advice as well as anything I may need that I did not have yet at the clinic. I will never forget when Larry told me this story. I hope you enjoy it as much as I did.

Larry had a small animal practice in a strip mall, with just one exam room and one surgery room. One day he was anesthetizing a cat for surgery. Using Ketamine, a common veterinary anesthetic back in the day, he attempted to inject the drug into the back leg of the cat. Ketamine, as most veterinarians know, is extremely painful when injected. Apparently, the cat found it to be most painful, for it jumped straight up, out of Larry's grasp, and latched on the drop ceiling tiles. At that split moment, the cat happened to have enough inertia to dislodge a ceiling tile and quickly scamper up into the ceiling.

My friend immediately grabbed a step ladder, hoisted himself up, and wedged his head into the missing ceiling tile's space. He spotted the cat crawling around on the ceiling tiles. Larry could tell, by how the cat was starting to tilt back and forth, that he must have gotten at least some of the Ketamine into the cat's back leg before it leapt to "safety." Patiently, he observed the cat for quite some time until it finally settled down, appearing to have fallen asleep atop a single ceiling tile.

The next step was determining exactly which tile in the ceiling the cat was sound asleep on. Larry started counting the number of tiles from where the cat had entered the ceiling to where it now lay. Having determined the approximate location, Larry went outside and then carried his step ladder into the greeting card shop next door. In the middle of a busy day, he calmly counted the ceiling tiles, set up his step ladder, moved a ceiling tile, reached up into the ceiling and pulled out what now appeared to be a dead cat. He gingerly replaced the ceiling tile and calmly carried the cat and step ladder out the door. I'm sure you can just imagine the looks on the faces of the owners and patrons of the card shop. Have a nice day. Don't mind the dead cat I am holding.

A LAST WORD FROM DR. ED:

Practice Makes Perfect

I have worked on this book off and on for most of my career, trying to write down the stories as soon as they happened so I would not forget. Of course, some came to me much later and I wrote from memory. I have had a very long and fruitful career, and recently sold my practice to my oldest daughter Anna and my son-in-law, Aaron. I am very proud of the fact that the clinic will remain a privately owned facility, and also remain in the family. As I write these words, my youngest daughter, Nina, has been accepted into the Royal Veterinary College of London. I could end up with two daughters as veterinarians. My middle daughter, Gina I am also proud to say, is a Doctor of Pharmacy, and plans to specialize in hematologic cancer treatment.

As I reach the beginning of the end of my career (though I still have some years left), I can reflect back on what has been a great blessing for me. I have been fortunate enough to work with not only my family, but with some of the greatest staff members ever to have worked at a veterinary clinic. I consider them all my family and will treasure their friendship forever. I have also been so lucky to get to help God's creatures every day that I have been a veterinarian. I truly believe that being a veterinarian was my purpose in life. I am blessed to have been able to follow my calling. And in helping my patients, I truly believe I have helped the owners and for that I am grateful.

Over the years I know and acknowledge that I have made my share of mistakes, both professionally and personally. I can honestly say that I have tried to learn from my mistakes and hopefully never repeat them. I believe that if a person does not learn from their mistakes, they are doomed to repeat them. Every day when I wake up, I look forward to work, knowing that it is going to be a great day, and that I have learned something from the previous day. After all, you know what they say. Practice makes perfect.

My three beautiful daughters, Nina, Gina and Anna (2023)

PRACTICE MAKES PERFECT

Acknowledgments

I have a lot of people to thank for their help in inspiring and helping to get this book to reality. First, I want to thank my family, especially my daughters, for inspiring me to want to be the best person I could be. I may have stumbled a few times over the years, but the thoughts of you three always brought me back. I have especially relished the opportunity to work side by side with my daughter Anna, and my son-in-law Aaron, as they have taken over the reins at Hillside Animal Hospital. I like to think that I built and ran a good veterinary clinic, but I am very proud of them as they have taken it to the next level and continue to run one of the best clinics in the area. I am very proud of my middle daughter Gina, who is now a Doctor of Pharmacy, and is a specialist working with cancer patients. My hat is off to you and the tough field you have chosen. I know you will excel as you have in everything you do. My youngest daughter Nina is now in veterinary school at the Royal College of Veterinary Medicine in London. I am enjoying watching you bloom as you work towards joining this great profession. I hope one day that we can also work side by side as colleagues. I want to thank all of my staff over the years, including but not limited to Jan Tarantola, Angie Davidson, Carrie Gravette, Matt Lang, Melissa Ravetta-Lang, Jamie Martin, and of course my very first employee, my Mom. My staff has always shared my passion and you all have made my career and life more interesting and fulfilling at the same time. I have had the privilege to work with some of the smartest and most dedicated veterinarians including but again not limited to Betsy Marziani, Micah Yuello, Mary Ann Bolser, and Tony Winkle. I am friends with some incredible veterinarians who have inspired me, helped me up when I was down, and laughed and cried

with me over the years, including Mark Lux, Dale Diesel, Ross Henry, Matt Sturmer, Will Cone, Marcy Hammerle, Linda Keon, Rae Anne Van Pelt, and Dave McGuffin. I have had multiple people help with editing over the years including Marie Fulcher, my future step daughter, Nicole Fulcher, my future wife, and Sharon Gambaro, a very close friend of many, many years. Thanks for catching all of my typos and for suggesting ways to make my writing sound better than it was. I would like to thank my collaborators on this project, Amanda Doyle, who is an accomplished author and gave me the confidence that I could pull this off, and Jill Halpin, who was fantastic in putting together the layout for the book. Both of these women started out as clients of mine, and later became collaborators and friends. Finally, I wish to thank all of the rescue groups I have either worked with in the past or continue to work with now. Besides giving me lots of material to inspire this book, you have offered me opportunities to grow professionally and learn more about veterinary medicine. A partial list of the rescue and not-for-profits organizations I have either volunteered for over the years include: Gateway Pet Guardians, Stray Rescue of St. Louis, Animal Protective Association of St. Louis, Carol House Quick Fix Pet Clinic, The Humane Society of Missouri, The Feral Companion, OPSPOT-St. Louis, Tenth Life Cat Rescue, Five Acres Animal Shelter, The Cat Network, Feline Friends, Pekin Duck Rescue, World Bird Sanctuary, English Springer Spaniel Rescue of America, Pound Pals, and Guardian Angel Bassett Rescue.

Finally, I would like to thank God for giving me the passion and intelligence to take care of his creatures, for blessing me with my children, and for allowing me to have a second chance at love.

Rescues

NATIONAL RESOURCES

ASPCA
424 E. 92nd St.
New York, NY 10128-6804
888-666-2279
Aspca.org

Maddie's Fund
6150 Stoneridge Mall Road, Suite 125
Pleasanton, CA 94588
925-310-5450
Maddiesfund.org

America Pets Alive
1156 Cesar Chavez St.
Austin, TX 78703
Americanpetsalive.org

Program for Pet Health Equity
1618 Cumberland Ave.
Knoxville, TN 37996
865-974-2809
pphe.utk.edu

**Veterinary Shelter
  Medicine Programs**
University of Florida
University of Wisconsin
University of California-Davis

LOCAL RESOURCES

Gateway Pet Guardians

725 N. 15th St.

East St. Louis, IL 62205

618-687-8007

Gatewaypets.org

Stray Rescue of St. Louis

2320 Pine St.

St. Louis, MO 63103

314-771-6121

Strayrescue.org

**Animal Protective Association
of Missouri**

1705 S. Hanley Rd.

St. Louis, MO 63144

314-645-4610

Apamo.org

Tenth Life Cat Rescue

3203 Cherokee St.

St. Louis, MO 63118

314-808-2454

Tenthlifecats.org

**OPSPOT (Operation Stop
Pet Overpopulation Today)**

PO Box 29563

St. Louis, 63127

314-95-8678

Opspot.org

Humane Society of Missouri

1202 Macklind Ave.

St. Louis, MO 63110

314-951-1562

Hsmo.org

The Feral Companion

Feralcompanion.org